Milk-Free
Diet Cookbook

Milk-Free Diet

Cookbook

Cooking for the Lactose Intolerant

Foreword by Eugene A. Gelzayd, M.D., F.A.C.P., F.A.C.G.

JANE ZUKIN

Sterling Publishing Co., Inc. New York

Distributed in the U.K. by Blandford Press

Dedicated with love and appreciation to my family, my friends and my doctors for their encouragement

Library of Congress Cataloging in Publication Data

Zukin, Jane.
  Milk-free diet cookbook.

  Includes index.
  1. Milk-free diet—Recipes. 2. Lactose
intolerance—Nutritional aspects. I. Title.
RM234.5.Z84   1981   641.5'632   81-8569
ISBN 0-8069-5566-X   AACR2
ISBN 0-8069-5567-8 (lib. bdg.)
ISBN 0-8069-7544-X (pbk.)

Third Printing, 1984

Copyright © 1982 by Jane Zukin
Published by Sterling Publishing Co., Inc.
Two Park Avenue, New York, N.Y. 10016
Distributed in Australia by Oak Tree Press Co., Ltd.
P.O. Box K514 Haymarket, Sydney 2000, N.S.W.
Distributed in the United Kingdom by Blandford Press
Link House, West Street, Poole, Dorset BH15 1LL, England
Distributed in Canada by Oak Tree Press Ltd.
c/o Canadian Manda Group, P.O. Box 920, Station U
Toronto, Ontario, Canada M8Z 5P9
Manufactured in the United States of America

Contents

Foreword

The author, a patient of mine, complained of bloating, abdominal cramps and diarrhea, off and on for a number of years and was treated for an acute infectious disease with antibiotics during a recent hospitalization. She was aware that lactose-containing products caused some of her symptoms. When we saw her in consultation, it was apparent from her medical history and test results that dairy products didn't agree with her. Simple institution of a strict lactose-free diet resulted in a full and lasting recovery.

Using her innate capability as a housewife and cook, and her knowledge concerning lactose-free products, she sensed that such a book should be written for patients with this problem—so common in the United States and throughout the world. The book should become a bible for every patient who complains of bloating, gas, abdominal distress or diarrhea following the ingestion of dairy products.

This work is timely, and the recipes are easy to follow. There is a good deal of nutritional and scientific information for the lay person to read and learn. Obviously, the author has a great deal of feeling in writing this book. The list of interesting foods that she prepared without lactose products makes this text unique and of considerable interest to any person with lactose intolerance. Let's hope that she will continue to update the scientific information and add more recipes. You see, I am looking ahead to the second edition already!

Eugene A. Gelzayd, M.D., F.A.C.P., F.A.C.G.
Chief, Section of Gastroenterology
Providence Hospital
Southfield, Michigan

Associate Clinical Professor of Medicine
Wayne State University School of Medicine
Detroit, Michigan

Preface

It's hard to believe that milk—so shrouded in love, nurturing and goodness—can adversely affect so many people. Yet, it is estimated that over 50 percent of the entire world's adult population cannot digest milk. In the United States alone, studies show that 30 million Americans are lactose-intolerant; 70 percent of the black population in the U.S. is intolerant to lactose. Other ethnic groups, including Japanese, Jews, Eskimos and South American Indians have exhibited a general intolerance to lactose.*

There are two types of milk sensitivity, the most common being an enzyme deficiency which hinders the hydrolysis of milk sugar. This is lactose intolerance. The other is an allergy to milk protein which may cause either allergic symptoms or intestinal disturbances like lactose intolerance. As a matter of fact, a prolonged intestinal disturbance itself can cause a lactose intolerance. Regardless of its type, the results are the same.

This book is devoted to the mainstream, that is, people with lactose intolerance. However, the diet and recipes given here omit all milk and milk by-products, so they are applicable to both milk-sugar and milk-protein intolerants.

* *Scientific American*, October 1972, p. 73.

Introduction

After my two sons were born, they had difficulty sleeping, writhed with intestinal pain, and had nonstop diarrhea. They had been through the usual battery of tests: Was it salmonella? Some mysterious bacteria? Celiac disease? Cystic fibrosis? All the results were negative. Finally, it was settled: Their suffering was due to lactose intolerance. My oldest son was switched to soy formula after two gruelling months of life. By the time my next son exhibited symptoms, the tests were done quickly. He was switched to soy formula at two weeks. So when my beautiful baby girl was born, I wasn't going to take any chances. Call it maturity, call it insight, but my intuition was firm: soy formula for Baby Girl Zukin.

The children grew and thrived on their milk-free diet. They didn't eat cheese slices, but they learned to love peanut butter. As they grew, all three eventually could tolerate milk in small amounts—even the baby, who was nursed for twelve months on soy formula, could later drink some milk.

My husband and I had so many questions about lactose intolerance. Where did it come from and why did all our children have it? Nowadays, milk-free formulas are in every corner drug store, but when our first two children were born, there wasn't as much widespread knowledge about lactose intolerance as there is now. We later found out that tolerance for milk is a subjective matter. Some children and adults can consume small amounts of plain milk as well as small amounts of milk in a fermented form such as yogurt, cottage cheese or sour cream. Digestion seems to be easier when milk products are consumed with other foods, at room temperature, or heated. Although these methods of preparation do not alter lactose levels appreciably, the resulting symptoms can be less severe.

Goat's milk can sometimes be tolerated because its lactose level is less than that of cow's milk. Also, sweet acidophilus milk is sometimes well tolerated because the lactobacillus acidophilus (a lactose-eating bacteria) has been added to lower the lactose level of the cow's milk.

With the passage of time, I found that the investigation into the causes and management techniques of lactose intolerance had grown.

Two recent studies shed new light on the lactose-intolerant condition. In a study performed under the direction of Dr. Albert D. Newcomer and associates of the Mayo Foundation, positive evidence emerged showing the close relationship between a deficiency of lactase (enzyme that breaks down lactose, the milk sugar) and genetic factors. The study focused on a Chippewa Indian community and came up with these results: Of 106 subjects tested, 78 percent were lactase-deficient. In families in which both parents were lactase-normal, 40 percent of the children were lactase-deficient. In families with one lactase-deficient parent, 65 percent of the children were lactase-deficient, and in families where both parents were lactase-deficient, 93 percent of the children were lactase-deficient. The evidence suggests a positive genetic factor.[*]

Another recently publicized theory about allergies reaches an important conclusion about the digestion of milk.[**] Dr. Lendon Smith, a noted pediatrician, talks about allergies and their relationship to milk. He notes that the adrenal glands of the body are the coping mechanism for secreting hormones that help the body control its reaction to foreign irritants. He recommends supplying the adrenal glands with vitamin C, pantothenic acid and B-complex vitamins. He also maintains that sugar and white flour cause the body's blood-sugar response to fluctuate to such a degree that it interferes with the normal adrenal response. These irritants, principally refined sugar, overload the system so that the body can't cope any longer, hence allergic symptoms emerge and take hold. Dr. Smith describes the typically "allergic" personality types and prescribes a combination of chemical relievers (medicine) and natural relievers (proper diet) to help the adrenal glands. He recommends the elimination of refined sugar and white flour, maintaining proper levels of vitamins and minerals, consuming frequent small meals, and eating protein rather than carbohydrate snacks. He also recommends the elimina-

[*] 1979 NIAMDD Research Advances, Digestive Diseases. Prepared by the National Institute of Arthritis, Metabolism and Digestive Diseases, Public Health Services, U.S. Dept. of Health, Education and Welfare, May 1979, pp. 11–12.
[**] Lendon Smith, Improving Your Child's Behavior Chemistry (Englewood Cliffs, New Jersey: Prentice-Hall, Inc., 1976), pp. 83–109.

tion of milk from the diet of the "allergic type" because he sees this as an unnecessary stress ingredient. If the body is already busy fighting foreign irritants, it does not need the added problem of dealing with the difficult task of digesting milk. If we sap the adrenal glands by the ingestion of milk, we won't have the necessary hormone levels to deal adequately with other foreign irritants.

Surely not in every case, but in most cases, people who maintain a proper blood-sugar level do attest to the merit of such a dietary program. Parents of hyperactive children who have had their diets changed, generally agree that controlling blood-sugar levels has a calming effect on their children. Adults who have been put on such a program also attest to the positive behavior and attitudinal changes that regulated blood-sugar levels deliver. In Ohio's Cuyahoga County, restricted diets are provided to juvenile offenders.

If it is true that lactose intolerance is hereditary, as Dr. Newcomer has concluded, then we can monitor our children for symptoms and limit their milk intake accordingly. If it is true that milk inhibits the body's natural ability to cope with allergic irritants, then we can expect some relief by eliminating milk from our diets. This must be done responsibly and under the supervision of a doctor who is knowledgeable about how food affects the body's reactions.

The responsibility does not end with the doctor, though. We cannot pass the buck when talking about a situation that requires our personal efforts with every meal. We must do our best to follow the lactose-free diet, not overdo our consumption of alcohol and caffeine (intestinal stimulants), and keep up with the news. Allergies and intolerances have so many and different kinds of symptoms, responses and treatments. It seems to me that the best way to know your tolerance level is through personal trial and error; only you know what foods make you ill. Keep lists and diaries and test yourself for food allergies at home.

How we feel about ourselves has to relate to how we care for ourselves. Obviously, if we believe that we are worthy of good health, we will strive for it. A four-year-old whom I recently met epitomizes the perception of a healthy child toward a lactose-intolerant lifestyle. Here was a little boy who vomited after eating or drinking milk products. Knowing that life at four is dotted with important social functions like birthday parties, I asked his mother if she would like a recipe for milk-free ice cream. She politely thanked me and declined the offer. Apparently, she had found a recipe for milk-free ice cream and made it for her son. He surprised her by refusing to eat it. It was so intensely ingrained in him that milk products would make him sick, that he wouldn't trust his mother enough to believe that the ice cream was truly milk-free. He knew what it felt like to be sick after meals, and he protected himself very carefully. There was no need to follow this little boy around or worry about his eating habits at a friend's house. He would not eat or drink any milk products anywhere, anytime, in any form, so long as it was recognizable to him. And, if something looked suspicious, he flatly declined to eat it. It didn't matter to him that he wasn't eating what other kids ate. It only mattered to him that he was well.

As adults, we are not always so sensible. Sometimes we know the risk and choose to take it anyway. Sometimes it's worth it, and sometimes it's not. After being stricken with a severe intestinal virus, for which I was hospitalized, I, too, was left totally lactose-intolerant. The test results revealed that I was probably somewhat lactose-intolerant all along. I went on a milk-free diet, but there was a day not too long ago when I temporarily went off my diet and slipped into an abyss of chocolate cookiedom. I had been feeling well for such a long time that I felt a favorite chocolate cookie would no longer hurt me. I knew there was a risk, but I was willing to take it. About fifteen cookies later, I felt so satisfied. About an hour and fifteen minutes later, I felt so sick. . . . Oh, well, it will be a long time before I take the risk again. It's back to the kitchen to try to work out a milk-free chocolate cookie recipe!

Changing eating habits is never easy. It is frustrating and difficult to pay such close attention to a part of life that had previously been taken for granted. Equally frustrating are the days when you seemingly do everything right regarding your diet and still get sick because lactose is hidden in something you are eating or drinking. The Food and Drug Administration (FDA) presently does not require the listing of *all* ingredients on consumable products and, therefore, lactose, a popular food and drug filler, may not be listed.

A digestive-system disorder, like lactose intolerance, can

have a powerful effect on your life-style, but it may be comforting to know you're not alone.

The National Institute of Arthritis, Metabolism, and Digestive Diseases, connected to the United States Department of Health, Education and Welfare (now known as the Department of Health and Human Services), had this to say about digestive disease:

> ... Disorders of the digestive system have serious impact and consequences. More Americans are hospitalized because of diseases of the digestive tract than for any other group of disorders. They rank second only to cardiovascular disease in the number of physician office visits or house calls ... Despite their considerable adverse impact and the consequent importance of studying these disorders, many of the digestive ailments remain poorly understood.*

Following my hospitalization, now knowing my body couldn't digest milk, I wondered what I would eat. So I went to work: I dusted off the cookbooks and started searching. I stormed down to the library and hauled home every book I could find on nutrition and food allergies. Next, I scouted the bookstores. "Have you a milk-free cookbook?" I asked over and over again. Maybe there was such a book, but I never found it.

So here, my friends, is the fruit of my labor. Here is a cookbook for those of us who will never sip the nectar of the cow. By virtue of the fact that you are reading this book, you are taking a positive step toward good health. You will become more proficient in determining a proper diet pattern for yourself or your child, and hopefully you will be relieved of some of the anxiety that might accompany your lactose-intolerant condition.

* 1979 NIAMDD Research Advances, Digestive Diseases, p. 1.

Questions and Answers about Lactose Intolerance

Most doctors recommend that the lactose-intolerant person pay close attention to his vitamin and mineral intake because certain nutrients the body needs are lacking when milk and milk products are eliminated from the diet. It has been proven that we don't need large amounts of fat or cholesterol in our diet, but we do need the protein, calcium and vitamin D that milk would normally provide.

Here are some answers to the most-often-asked questions about lactose intolerance and the vitamins and minerals specifically needed in the diet of the lactose-intolerant person.

What are the symptoms of lactose intolerance?

Symptoms and their severity vary from person to person. Generally, people with lactose intolerance will have abdominal pain, cramping, a bloated or "belchy" feeling and diarrhea. Diarrhea brings with it side effects such as rectal tenderness, bodily weakness, dehydration and weight loss. These symptoms are noted probably within an hour of ingesting milk or can be noted up to several days afterward, depending on the individual's tolerance level. Some people get skin eruptions or eczema; some have to be hospitalized. Though the degree of intensity of symptoms is enormous, abdominal distress is the common denominator.

How do I know for sure if I have it?

After reporting your symptoms to your doctor, he will probably run some tests. He will run stool cultures to determine if there is a bacterial infection and might also conduct tests to eliminate various malabsorption diseases (diseases in which normal absorption of nutrients is impaired). There are several types of bacterial or malabsorption conditions that

11

cause lactose intolerance, though often, none of these are present.* The next step is a lactose-intolerance test which determines the extent of the lactase enzyme deficiency. This enzyme must be present to digest lactose, and the test gives an indication of the amount of lactase absent in the body. The test is quite easy to take: One pint of pure lactose is ingested, followed by two hours of glucose level measurement. In other words, you drink the "sugar water" and have your blood drawn four times in two hours. A lactase deficiency is positively identified if the blood glucose level fails to rise above the fasting level. When lactose enters the intestines, the enzyme lactase is released and breaks down lactose into glucose and galactose. From there, the liver changes the galactose into glucose. If all goes according to plan, the glucose would then travel into the bloodstream and elevate the fasting glucose level. If absorption is incomplete, the blood glucose level does not rise sufficiently, if at all. Hence, a lactose intolerance is confirmed. The patient will usually show some abdominal distress within that two-hour period.

Lactase activity is high at birth in most humans, but generally declines during childhood. Many lactose-intolerant children show lessened symptoms during adolescence, though resurgence of symptoms can occur during the teen years. We all have decreased lactase activity in later life, so most older adults should decrease their milk (but not calcium) intake.

If you are not exhibiting symptoms but are curious about your tolerance to lactose, an easy way to test yourself can be done at home. Do not eat for several hours and then drink three or four large glasses of milk. If you get diarrhea or cramping, you have at least some intolerance. This is by no means an accurate measure and is not a replacement for the lactose-intolerance test, but is helpful in determining whether lactose intolerance runs in your family.

What is lactose?

Simply put, lactose is milk sugar. It is a disaccharide (a double sugar), composed of glucose and galactose; it is split into its two simple sugars by digestive enzymes. It is the only sugar of animal origin of significance in man's diet. The concentration of lactose in milk varies from 2 to 8 percent, de-

* Barium X rays may be taken to rule out other disorders.

pending on the animal. Human milk contains almost twice as much lactose as cow's milk. Lactose is generally added to prepared infant formulas to make up this difference. Lactose is the carbohydrate of milk; fats, proteins and water are milk's other components.

What is lactose intolerance?

If there is a deficiency or absence of a specific enzyme in the body, digestion is incomplete. In this case, the enzyme lactase is either not present in the intestinal mucosa or is not present in sufficient amounts. There are two types of lactase deficiencies: Primary lactase deficiency is a congenital absence of the lactase enzyme in the digestive system; secondary lactase deficiency is an acquired absence of the lactase enzyme, which often results after bouts with bacterial or viral infections.

In the absence of the enzyme lactase, lactose is not broken down into glucose and galactose. The accumulation of lactose in the intestines causes fermentation, abdominal pain, cramping, diarrhea and oftentimes weight loss. People with a chronic diarrhea problem (like those suffering from ileitis, colitis or irritable bowel syndrome) are advised to eliminate milk from their diet. The diarrhea itself depletes the intestines of lactase. This is an example of secondary lactase deficiency caused by a chronic digestive disease.

Why do I need calcium, and how do I get sufficient amounts of it?

Calcium is very important for our health. It has been designated as a component of stress: A severe lack of calcium can cause nervousness and irritability. For children, it is vital for bone and teeth formation, and in later years is vital for their proper health. Calcium must have vitamins D, A, C and phosphorus in order to function, so all these nutrients must be accounted for in the diet. Unfortunately, the prime sources of calcium are milk and cheese. Other food sources are inadequate; therefore, calcium supplements are the solution. Excess calcium that is unabsorbed is released through perspiration, urine and the bowel. However, proper amounts of calcium differ for each individual, so do not attempt to supplement your diet or that of your child without first consulting your doctor.

The Food and Nutrition Board, National Academy of Sciences, National Research Council, sets the minimum daily requirements (MDR) of vitamins and minerals for adults and children over four years of age. Since requirements for infants are different from those for adults, check with your doctor. A more complete vitamin and mineral MDR table is at the back of the book.

In order to determine whether or not you are receiving the appropriate amounts of calcium and vitamin D in your diet, check your daily vitamin supplement, your enriched breads and cereals, or any other food that is premeasured and that you consume daily. For infants and children who may be drinking soy formula as a milk substitute, add up the amounts of calcium and vitamin D used daily, including amounts used in daily cooking. If the minimum daily requirements are not being met, supplement with OS CAL, or calcium gluconate, dolomite, calcium lactate, NEO-CAL glucose liquid or other calcium supplement.

Vitamin D requirements are generally fulfilled through an over-the-counter daily multivitamin tablet. I prefer to buy only natural vitamin and mineral supplements. Sometimes lactose fillers are added to capsules or vitamin pills, so always read the labels and check with your pharmacist.

What are good sources of vitamin D?

Vitamin D regulates the absorption of calcium and phosphorus and aids in the calcification of bones and teeth. Foods are poor sources of vitamin D, though small amounts are found in eggs, fish and meat. People used to take it in the form of cod-liver oil, but nowadays it is fortified milk that supplies our daily requirements. Without milk in the diet, a supplement is recommended. Vitamin D is sometimes called the sunshine vitamin because exposure of the body to sunlight will convert a substance in the skin to vitamin D. Excesses of vitamin D can be toxic, so don't use supplements without medical advice.

Which foods are good sources of vitamin C?

Luckily, vitamin C (ascorbic acid) is readily available in many foods. Vitamin C has been proven to promote healthy bone and tooth formation because it works with calcium. It

14

has been said to give us energy, stimulate the appetite, raise our resistance to infection and strengthen the blood vessels. However, one thing about vitamin C is certain: The body does not make vitamin C, nor does it store it for more than a few hours. We need a new supply every day, and throughout the day. The best sources of vitamin C are citrus fruits and juices such as orange, grapefruit and grape.

What is carotene, and why do I need it?

Carotene is the yellow pigment in plants. The carotenes in foods are converted by the body into vitamin A, which is involved in many vital processes. It is very important for our eyes and is a "membrane conditioner" in that it keeps the mucous linings of the body in good condition. This is important for the digestive system. For those of us who suffer intestinal upsets, the health of this area is enhanced by proper levels of vitamin A. Vitamin A also aids in the secretion of gastric juices and in the digestion of protein. In animal tissue (meat), vitamin A is primarily found in the liver. Carotene, however, is plentiful in carrots, spinach, sweet potatoes, winter squash, apricots, broccoli, pumpkins, cantaloupes, romaine lettuce, kale and collard greens, endive, avocados, artichokes and nectarines.

In order to preserve the high levels of carotene in foods, food preparation is important. Fruits and vegetables do not lose carotene when eaten raw or when steamed. Dried fruits and vegetables lose about half of their vitamin content in the dehydration process, while frying totally destroys it. Vitamin A and carotene can be toxic when taken to excess. Your doctor can test your carotene level through a special blood test and determine how much of it you need.

What about fibre?

The importance of fibre in the diet is generally recognized, but only you and your doctor can determine how much fibre your body needs or can tolerate. However, whereas fibre had been routinely eliminated from the diet of people suffering from intestinal disturbances, this is no longer the case.

Studies show that fibre acts positively on the digestive system in two ways. It increases the transit time for elimination, thus releasing unabsorbed or detrimental (carcinogenic) material more quickly, lessening the damage such material can cause. Fibre also increases the bulk of the stool. Consequently, more fecal matter is released, thereby producing a cleansing action on the inestinal linings.

Ask your doctor how much and what types of fibre you should eat. Fibre refers to the skins, seeds and structural parts of plant foods and includes raw fruit and vegetables, bran and nuts. One important element to remember about the digestion of fibre is proper chewing. If the teeth are in poor condition or absent, juicing or pulverizing is helpful, especially when feeding your lactose-intolerant baby. You can then gradually add fruit and vegetable skins to your infant's diet.

Are other vitamins important?

When speaking about daily requirements, it is necessary to include the vitamin B-complex family. Though the role of these vitamins is not completely known, it has been proven that they are necessary for metabolic changes within the cell structure and are involved in the breakdown of carbohydrates, proteins and fats in the body. These vitamins aid in the breakdown of lactose into glucose and galactose.

Many of the B-complex vitamins, such as thiamine, riboflavin and niacin, are added to enriched breads and cereals. Folic acid, which is important for cell production, and vitamin B-12, which has been used to fight against pernicious anemia and sprue (a malabsorption disease), are also added to many fortified products. However, fortified milk is the largest provider of the B-complex vitamins in the average American diet. Any good over-the-counter vitamin tablet will fulfill the B-complex requirements for the lactose-intolerant. Vitamin B is water-soluble and is eliminated through the urine when the body no longer needs it.

Minimum daily requirements of additional vitamins and minerals can be found in the tables at the back of the book. Basically, the essential nutrients required daily are:

Water-soluble vitamins— ascorbic acid (vitamin C) and B-complex vitamins listed as thiamine, riboflavin, niacin, pantothenic acid, biotin, B-6, B-12, and folic acid (folacin)

Fat-soluble vitamins—vitamins A, D, E, K

Minerals—calcium, phosphorus, magnesium, potassium

Trace elements—iron, iodine, zinc, manganese, copper, chromium

The Lactose-Free Diet

The basic principles behind a lactose-free diet are quite simple: If there is no lactase in the body, no lactose should be eaten; if there is some lactase in the body, some lactose can be eaten and digested. Only you can determine how much lactose you can tolerate and in what form. Start by eliminating all lactose from the diet and, perhaps in a month, add baked products with lactose. If you can tolerate these, work your way up to aged cheeses like Cheddar or Swiss. Next, try yogurt (some of the lactose is predigested by the bacteria). If you have a setback, begin again. I tried a teaspoon of cheese, six months after totally eliminating lactose from my diet, and got sick, but this would not necessarily happen to everyone.

The foods listed in the lactose-free diet are starting points for menu-building. Brand-name products are listed at the beginning of each chapter with the exception of some categories that have lists too long to mention.

Following is a list of foods you would do best to avoid, though not everyone who is lactose-intolerant must eliminate all of these in their diet. As mentioned previously, your level of tolerance for lactose will determine what foods you should not eat.

Foods You Cannot Eat

Dairy

butter, margarine
cheese and cheese dishes (e.g., macaroni & cheese)
creamed eggs and omelets
milk in all forms (including powdered, evaporated, malted, condensed and dried milk and milk solids, whole and skim milk, cultured or buttermilk)
cream, sour cream
yogurt
artificial sour cream and cream cheese
curds and whey

Baking products

coating mixes for fried chicken
prepared mixes for sweets, breads, pie crust, waffles

Foods You Cannot Eat (continued)

Potatoes

au gratin, instant, scalloped

Meats

breaded or creamed meat
cold cuts containing milk
prepared meats (including mixed cuts such as "hamburger")
sausage products (Check for milk fillers.)

Soups

bisques
canned soups
chowder
cream soups

Miscellaneous

beverages made with milk (cocoa, eggnog)
gravies, sauces (canned)
salad dressings (creamed)
vegetables (buttered)
vitamin capsules and medications using lactose fillers

Baked goods

breads & crackers made with milk
cakes & cookies made with milk solids
crackers, biscuits ⎤
doughnuts   ⎬ store-bought
muffins   ⎦
pancakes, waffles

Desserts

Bavarian cremes
custard, puddings
ice cream, sherbet
junkets
milk-chocolate candy
mousse
patisserie

Other

milk proteins (casein, sodium caseinate, lactalbumin)

You may eat the following foods, all approved brands mentioned in each chapter, and all kosher-pareve products:

Foods You Can Eat

Milk-free margarines *
DIET IMPERIAL
MANESCHEWITZ
MARV-PARV
MAZOLA salt-free
MOTHER'S
PURITY
WEIGHT WATCHERS

Milk substitutes
DAIRY WHIP
HUNT'S REDDI-WHIP (nondairy)
RICH'S RICH WHIP
RICH'S COFFEE RICH
WHITEHOUSE PRESTO WHIP

Candies
fruit candy
hard candy
jelly beans
licorice
marshmallows

Baked goods
angel food cake
breads (on approved list)
crackers (on approved list)
homemade
sponge cake

Miscellaneous
chocolate syrup (BOSCO, HERSHEY'S)
eggs
fruit
gelatin desserts
honey
jams, jellies
syrups
vegetables (fresh, frozen; no sauce)

* The following can be used in all recipes in this book that require milk-free margarine.

Foods You Can Eat (continued)

Meat/Seafood

beef/veal
fish
lamb
pork (ham and sausage products without milk fillers)
poultry
seafood

Soups

bouillon
consommé
homemade

Condiments

ketchup
mayonnaise
mustard
relish

Baking products

baking chocolate (dark only—no German chocolate)
brown sugar
carob powder
cocoa powder (plain)
semisweet morsels (NESTLÉS, HERSHEY'S)
sugar (granulated, powdered)

Starches

pastas
potatoes } no milk/cheese sauce
rice

Beverages

carbonated drinks
coffee (includes decaffeinated)
tea
fruit drinks

NOTE: Kosher dietary rules prohibit the mixing of milk and meat products. An item that is labeled "pareve" means that it can be eaten at either a dairy or a meat meal; therefore, it contains no milk.

How to Read a Food Label

There are many federal regulations governing the information on a food label. Ingredients listed on food labels are in descending order of predominance; in other words, the first ingredient listed comprises the largest amount of the product, while the last ingredient listed comprises the least. Percentages are not always given and are not required to be on the label. Some labels are more informative than others because the manufacturer has voluntarily decided to disclose more information than is required. That helps those of us who are looking out for particular ingredients. Certain products can use optional ingredients that do not have to appear on the label—and lactose may be one of those that is not listed in foods—which include the following:

cocoa products
flour
macaroni and noodle products
white bread and rolls
enriched bread and rolls
raisin bread and rolls
whole wheat bread and rolls
milk and cream
natural cheeses
processed cheeses
frozen desserts
food flavorings
salad dressing
canned fruit and juice
fruit pies
fruit butters, jellies and preserves
nonalcoholic beverages
canned vegetables

When reading labels, check for (and avoid) milk and milk by-products (for more information, see pp. 17—18). Sometimes the lactose-intolerant person is sensitive to milk protein as well, so casein, lactalbumin and sodium caseinate must also be avoided. Sometimes even beef must be avoided, though the reason for sensitivity to beef in a lactose-intolerant person is not yet known.

Caring for the Lactose-Intolerant Infant

If your baby has had diarrhea for a long time and lactose intolerance has been determined to be the cause, there are many things you can do to nurse your baby back to health. Pay attention to the baby's stools and notice whether they are loose or watery, or if mucus is present. Report any changes to your doctor and don't be embarrassed to discuss stool information with him because it is a good indication of your baby's progress. If your baby was not previously gaining weight, weight gain should be forthcoming.

Omit lactose from your baby's formula by switching to a soy formula or predigested formula; your doctor can advise you about which is best for your baby. The second step is often to dilute the new formula for the first week or so and then gradually build up to full strength. Increased amounts of water are necessary for digestive distress recovery.

Do not feed your baby solid foods. If he was eating cereal or fruit, stop these altogether. The digestive system needs time to recover from a bout of diarrhea, and solid foods only tax the system more. More frequent bottle feedings may be necessary, but this will give the baby not only the nourishment he needs, but the liquid replacement he requires as well. After the stools return to normal, begin feeding solid foods again. Give only one type of food at a time, in small amounts, to start. After three or four days of formed stools on the first solid food, add another and continue introducing foods in this slow and methodical manner. You will then be able to determine which foods, if any, might cause your baby to suffer from intestinal distress.

Note which foods are easy for your baby to digest, as well as those that cause him discomfort. By keeping a feeding record, you will have done yourself, the doctor and your child a large favor.

Many pediatricians are beginning to change their thoughts on the introduction of solid foods and are advising that solids not be introduced until the baby is between four and six months of age. So don't worry if your baby is not taking solid foods until then. Some pediatricians go one step farther and do not permit milk during the first year of life.

It has been proven that beginning an infant on breast milk is the best way of protecting him from allergies and intolerances. Rarely, but possibly, the baby will not be able to tolerate the amount of lactose in breast milk. Perhaps you could find a happy medium by breast-feeding twice a day and supplementing with lactose-free formula the rest of the time. You will have to express the breast milk during supplemental feeding time, but the baby will receive some breast milk and the benefit of natural feeding.

While your baby is uncomfortable, he will need more loving, stroking, rocking and holding than usual. Don't worry about "spoiling" him. Remember that he is in pain and needs your love and attention to help him feel better and thrive. When the pain subsides (and this can take a few weeks) he should be happier, more relaxed and content. The pediatrician who cared for my second child was convinced that he gained weight strictly on hugs because he certainly wasn't keeping much formula down!

One trick I learned is to prepare a type of heating pad for times when your baby feels especially uncomfortable. Get your hands on a hot-water bottle and fill it with warm, not hot, water. The water should be warm to the forearm. Place the hot-water bottle on your lap and cover it with a cloth diaper, receiving blanket or thin towel. Lay the baby across your lap on this infant-sized heating pad and gently swing your legs from side to side. Chances are he'll be asleep soon.

Some babies are more comfortable on your shoulder, with their knees bent and your hand supporting their feet. The key is to find what works for your child and stick with it. Making him as comfortable as possible is really important, and he will reward you in ways that only babies can.

Having been involved with lactose intolerance as both a parent and a "victim," I have developed an attitude toward the condition which is based on both experiences. Parents of lactose-intolerant infants have the burden thrust upon them from the earliest moments of parenthood. Most new parents are apprehensive, somewhat nervous, and most certainly in the throes of a new and difficult adjustment. Healthy babies demand a great deal from parents; greater demand is placed on them if they have a lactose-intolerant infant. If you are the grandparent or a family friend, recognize that parents of a lactose-intolerant infant need your support, so when babysitting, ask what you should do if the baby is uncomfortable and what position is best for bottle-feeding and burping.

Special Help for Children and Adults

If you or your child have just acquired lactose intolerance, keep in mind that it will take a couple of weeks for your distress to totally abate. Be sure to eliminate all sources of lactose from the diet for now. If you suffer from diarrhea, follow this eating course:

1. Eliminate solid foods from the diet.

2. Put yourself or your child on a liquid diet that includes broth, gelatin, fruit and vegetable juice, soft drinks, bouillon, weak tea and decaffeinated coffee. Be sure to include orange juice and beef broth as part of a daily liquid regimen. These are rich in potassium, a vital mineral which is depleted from the body during a long siege of diarrhea. Potassium depletion will make you feel weak, listless and apprehensive.

3. Continue this regimen until a stool begins to form.

4. Slowly add foods to your diet, beginning with breads and cereals, rice, potatoes (without butter on top) or eggs that aren't fried.

5. Steamed vegetables and light meats like fish, chicken or turkey can be added next.

6. Slowly work your way up to raw fruits and vegetables.

7. Next add other meats and dishes comprised of a combination of foods.

Don't tax your digestive system when you have diarrhea, since it needs time to recuperate. You may reach a point where you can recover quite quickly from an episode, perhaps within 24 hours. Later, you may experiment with small amounts of milk products to find your healthy tolerance level. Some people can eat cottage cheese, yogurt and aged cheeses like Cheddar and Swiss.

Chances are the whole family is not lactose-intolerant: In many situations, only one member of the family is in need of daily management. This needn't throw off the entire eating arrangement if some attention is paid to advance preparation. Let's face it, it is not fun to prepare two meals for every breakfast, lunch and dinner, so here are a few hints to make mealtime more pleasant at your house.

1. Keep an ample supply of staples on hand, such as packages of milk-free margarine and several kinds of milk-free breads, all of which freeze well for months.

2. When preparing a milk-free dish, package the leftovers

in individual wrappings and freeze for a later single serving at lunchtime or dinner when it's pizza night for some members of the family.

3. Stock up on milk-free bread and freeze in plastic bags. Limit each bag to about eight slices of bread. That way the bread will stay fresh until you get to the end of the loaf.

4. Wrap some muffins, brownies or cake slices individually. These can be frozen and thrown into a brown bag or lunchbox as needed and no thawing is necessary.

5. Instead of making half a gallon of ice cream, try molding ices in individual containers. They will stay fresher longer.

6. Set aside a certain time each month to prepare some milk-free dishes for the freezer. Then, when you don't feel like cooking and the family is going to eat grilled-cheese sandwiches, the lactose-intolerant person has something to eat that's easy to serve.

7. Find a kosher bakery. Even if it's not in your neighborhood, it is well worth a trip every now and then. You can stock up on items for the freezer. In a strictly kosher bakery, all items are pareve and contain no milk products. Hamburger and hot dog buns can be found there and can be wrapped and frozen in plastic bags for several months, as can other baked goods.

8. Search out your local health-food stores for a product called "LACT-AID." This is a liquid enzyme that is poured into a quart of milk. It breaks down the lactose by about 75% or, doubled, up to 90%. Some people can tolerate lactose at this level; it is worth a try.

9. When invited to a friend's home for dinner, always offer to bring a dish you've made. That way you'll know there will be at least one milk-free dish served at the meal and your friend will have less special preparation to do.

10. Be sure your child's friends know that he doesn't drink milk. Pack him a milk-free goody when he's visiting, so he won't feel left out at snack time.

11. When selecting a restaurant, choose a place that cooks fresh food daily. Don't be shy about asking questions concerning how certain dishes are prepared. But don't take anything for granted, either: Tell the waitress that you are not to have any milk products in your meal. If you get the French bread buttered anyway, just smile and ask for a new piece.

12. A word about medications: Lactose is used as a filler in many medicines. Before taking any prescription drug, ask your pharmacist to give you a list of ingredients in the pills or capsules or check with your doctor. Also check all labels of vitamin tablets or other over-the-counter preparations before taking them. If you have difficulty finding the lactose content of pills, call or write the pharmaceutical company. Lactose is used as a filler in many medications, but the FDA does not require that it be listed on the label.

13. Lactose-intolerant toddlers and small children are in the midst of a "no-no" life that has a larger negative scope than normal. In addition to not touching plugs and television knobs, they must not eat the ice cream from the ice-cream man. They can only have a homemade iced fudge stick when a milk shake is what they really want. The person who prepares their meals should be able to provide enough diversity and excitement in their foods. Let your child help himself to approved snacks and see to it that unapproved foods are less enticing. If ice cream is the only treat in the freezer, it looks very good to a two-year-old who has learned how to open the door. But, if he knows that the homemade iced fudge sticks were made especially for him and that he can help himself, they will probably look just as good as the ice cream.

Abbreviations Used in This Book

Customary Terms

t.	teaspoon
T.	tablespoon
c.	cup
pkg.	package
pt.	pint
qt.	quart
oz.	ounce
lb.	pound
°F	degrees Fahrenheit
in.	inch
env.	envelope

Metric Symbols

mL	millilitre
L	litre
g	gram
kg	kilogram
mm	millimetre
cm	centimetre
°C	degrees Celsius

About the Recipes

Digestibility is at the top of the list of my priorities. Therefore, the recipes in this cookbook are comprised of milk-free foods that are natural for the most part. They are seasoned lightly with nonirritating spices and none are fried. What you will find is a blend of plain and fancy dishes that are delicious, nutritious and milk-free. I hope you will enjoy them and add them to your list of tried-and-true milk-free favorites.

At the beginning of each chapter, I have included a list of brand-name products that are milk-free. I can make these recommendations based on the product's labeling and can only hope that the manufacturers have listed the ingredients properly. You can make a list of brand-name products that are available only in your area, as the products I have listed are generally available nationally.

NOTE: The brand names mentioned are for the reader's convenience. They are not all natural or chemical-free foods and should not be construed as such. I personally use very few prepared products, so I cannot vouch for their quality.

APPETIZERS AND BEVERAGES

Appetizers

Look for these prepared and packaged milk-free hors d'oeuvres: MA COHEN'S kosher products, which include miniature hot dogs wrapped in dough and miniature turkey franks; EMPIRE kosher meats, including a party pack of prepared fried chicken, Chinese egg rolls and other party snacks. The recipes in the first part of this chapter normally call for cream cheese or sour cream as a binder. In these milk-free versions, eggs, mayonnaise and wine have been used instead.

Stuffed Cherry Tomatoes

24	cherry tomatoes	24
7-oz. can	white tuna fish (drained)	198 g
2 T.	mayonnaise	30 mL
1 T.	pickle relish	15 mL
6-oz. can	black olives (pitted)	170 g

Rinse and drain the tomatoes. Cut off the tops; scoop out and discard the seeds. In a small bowl, mix tuna, mayonnaise and relish. Stuff each tomato with tuna mixture. Slice enough olives to make 24 slices; top each tomato with a piece of olive.
Yield: 24 stuffed cherry tomatoes

Stuffed Mushrooms

1 lb.	fresh mushrooms	450 g
2 T.	chives, chopped	30 mL
2 T.	milk-free margarine	30 mL
2	eggs (beaten)	2
2 t.	salt	10 mL
1 t.	pepper	5 mL
1 t.	garlic powder	5 mL
	Milk-Free Bread Crumbs (p. 38–39)	

Rinse mushrooms and pat dry with paper toweling. Remove stems and chop; set aside the caps. Sauté chives and chopped stems in margarine for 1 minute. Put this mixture in a small bowl, add eggs, salt, pepper and garlic powder. Blend thoroughly. Spoon mixture into mushroom caps and sprinkle with bread crumbs. Place mushrooms on an ungreased cookie sheet. Bake at 425 °F (218 °C) for about 15 minutes or until bread crumbs are browned.

Yield: About 12–20 stuffed mushrooms

NOTE: These stuffed mushrooms may be prepared in advance and baked just before serving.

Caviar Pie

6	eggs (hard-boiled)	6
1 T.	mayonnaise	15 mL
two 2- to 3-oz. jars	caviar	two 57- to 85-g jars
½ c.	red onion, chopped	125 mL

Chop eggs thoroughly and mix with just enough mayonnaise to hold chopped eggs together. Press gently into a 6-in. (15-cm) springform pan. Refrigerate for several hours or overnight. Remove outside of pan and place egg mould on a serving dish. Spread top with a thin layer of mayonnaise, then a layer of caviar. Sprinkle with chopped onion. Refrigerate until serving time.

Yield: 4 servings

Chinese Chicken Crepes

1 c.	chicken (cooked and finely chopped)	250 mL
½ c.	mushrooms, chopped	125 mL
2 T.	green pepper, chopped	30 mL
1 T.	tomato, chopped	15 mL
1 T.	onion, chopped	15 mL
2	eggs (beaten)	2
½ t.	salt	3 mL
¼ t.	white pepper	1.5 mL
	vegetable oil	
18 small	Crepes (p. 41)	18 small
	Sweet and Sour Sauce (recipe below)	

Combine chicken, mushrooms, green pepper, tomato and onion. Add beaten eggs to chicken mixture, then mix in salt and pepper. Put 1½ T. (25 mL) of mixture on cooked side of each crepe. Fold in sides and roll up. Place filled crepes on an ungreased cookie sheet; brush with oil. Bake at 400 °F (205 °C) for 15 to 20 minutes, or until browned. Top with sauce.
Yield: 18 crepes

Sweet and Sour Sauce

½ c.	chili sauce	125 mL
½ c.	grape jelly	125 mL
2 T.	lemon juice	10 mL
½ c.	soy sauce	125 mL

Put all ingredients in a small saucepan and stir to mix. Bring to boil, then lower the heat and simmer for 15 minutes.
Yield: About 1½ c. (375 mL) sauce, enough for 18 crepes

Anchovy Puffs

	Plain Pastry (p. 93)	
2-oz. can	anchovies	57 g

Mash anchovies and blend into pastry mixture. Roll to ¼-in. (6-mm) thickness. Cut into squares or any other shape. Place on an ungreased cookie sheet. Bake at 450 °F (230 °C) for 10 minutes, or until puffs are nicely browned.
Yield: About 24

Egg Salad Mould

1 pkg.	unflavored gelatin	1 pkg.
½ c.	cold water	125 mL
1 t.	salt	5 mL
1 t.	lemon juice	5 mL
½ t.	Worcestershire sauce	3 mL
3 drops	hot sauce	3 drops
¾ c.	mayonnaise	180 mL
1½ t.	onion, chopped	8 mL
¼ c.	green pepper, chopped	60 mL
4 to 6	eggs (hard-boiled)	4 to 6

Sprinkle gelatin over cold water in medium saucepan. Place over low heat and stir constantly until gelatin dissolves. Remove from heat and add salt, lemon juice, Worcestershire sauce and hot sauce. Cool this mixture. Stir in mayonnaise, onion and green pepper. Chop eggs; add them to the mixture and gently mix well. Turn into a 3-cup (750-mL) mould and chill until firm.
Yield: 3 c. (750 mL)

Chopped Liver (Pâté)

2 small	onions (sliced)	2 small
1 T.	milk-free margarine	15 mL
1 lb.	chicken livers	450 g
	salt and pepper to taste	
3	eggs (hard-boiled)	3
2 T.	port wine	30 mL

Sauté the onions in milk-free margarine until transparent; set aside. Rinse livers in cold water and drain. Place them on a broiler pan and sprinkle with salt and pepper. Broil livers on a low rack at 500 °F (260 °C), turning them to broil all sides. When cooked, use either a food processor or a meat grinder to blend the chicken livers, eggs and sautéed onions. Mix in the wine and adjust the seasoning if necessary.
Yield: 8 servings

Shrimp Croustades

16 slices	milk-free bread	16 slices
	Shrimp Filling (recipe below)	
	milk-free margarine	
	Milk-Free Bread Crumbs (p. 38–39)	

Cut out 16 rounds of milk-free bread with the top of a 3-in. (7.5-cm) glass. (Reserve the crusts for making bread crumbs.) Place rounds in the cups of a muffin pan and press them into shape. Bake at 375 °F (190 °C) for 10 minutes. Remove toasted rounds and place them on a cookie sheet. Fill each round with a hefty spoonful of Shrimp Filling. Top with a dot of milk-free margarine and sprinkle with bread crumbs. Bake at 450 °F (230 °C) for 10 minutes or until toasted. Serve hot.

NOTE: The croustades and filling can be made ahead of time. Refrigerate the filling; the croustades do not need refrigeration. Fill and bake just before serving.

Shrimp Filling

8-oz. bag	tiny frozen shrimp,	227-g bag
or	cooked	or
2 c.	fresh shrimp cooked and chopped	500 mL
3 T.	mayonnaise	45 mL
3 T.	chili sauce	45 mL
1½ T.	onion, minced	25 mL
8 drops	hot sauce	8 drops
2 T	celery, minced	30 mL
2 t.	lemon juice	10 mL

Thaw frozen shrimp by placing bag under cold running water. Check that all the veins have been removed. If using fresh-cooked shrimp, chop into ½-in. (1-cm) pieces. Toss shrimp with other ingredients.

Yield: 16 croustades

Stuffed Celery

15-oz can	salmon	425 g
2	eggs (hard-boiled and chopped)	2
	mayonnaise	
	salt and pepper to taste	
10 stalks	celery (washed and trimmed)	10 stalks

Rinse and drain salmon; remove any bones. Mix salmon with half the chopped egg and enough mayonnaise to be well-moistened. Add salt and pepper. Cut celery stalks in half and fill each stalk with salmon mixture. Sprinkle remaining chopped egg on top.

Yield: 20 stalks of stuffed celery

Many appetizers do not call for milk at all. Instead, they make use of fresh fruits and vegetables, including mashed avocados as a base. There is lots of room for imagination with these nonmilk starters.

Guacamole

2	avocados (pitted and peeled)	2
1 T.	onion, grated	15 mL
1 T.	lemon juice	15 mL
1 t.	salt	5 mL
⅓ c.	mayonnaise	85 mL

Mash avocados with a fork. Blend in other ingredients and mix well. Chill. Serve with crackers, pretzels or breadsticks.

Yield: 1 c. (250 mL)

VARIATIONS: Add chopped shrimp, clams, cucumber, bell pepper or tomato. Guacamole is versatile; many different dips can be created using it as the base.

33

Sardine Dip

two 4½-oz. cans	sardines (smoked, skinless, boneless)	two 128-g cans
½ c.	mayonnaise	125 mL
1 t.	prepared mustard	5 mL

Mash sardines in a small bowl. Add mayonnaise and mustard and blend well. Serve very cold.
Yield: About 1 c. (250 mL)

Skewered Fruit or Vegetables

Cut a variety of fruits or vegetables into good-sized chunks. Put them on small skewers or toothpicks and arrange on a tray. Serve with powdered sugar for the fruit, or a dip for the vegetables. Try any of the following combinations:

Fruit Combinations

- Honeydew
- Cantaloupe
- Papaya
- Strawberries

- Apples
- Tangerines
- Pears
- Cherries

- Seedless green grapes
- Watermelon
- Fresh peaches
- Pineapple

Vegetable Combinations

- Raw carrots
- Raw cauliflower
- Raw zucchini

- Celery
- Steamed beets
- Cut sugar pea pods

- Canned hearts of palm
- Watercress
- Pearl onions

Beverages

When preparing beverages in a blender, juice or fruit mixed with ice cubes delivers the same frothiness as milk. A milk substitute can also be used.

Holiday Punch

two 46-oz. cans	pineapple juice	two 1.3-kg cans
46-oz. can	orange juice	1.3 kg
1 qt.	ginger ale	1 L
half-gallon	Light Strawberry Ice Cream (p. 100)	2 L
	orange and lime slices for garnish	

Put all ingredients in a punch bowl and stir. Add ice, and garnish with orange and lime slices.
Yield: 12–20 servings

Hot Cocoa

½ c.	milk substitute	125 mL
½ c.	water	125 mL
1½ t.	cocoa powder	8 mL
¾ t.	sugar	4 mL
	marshmallow (optional)	

Put all ingredients in a small saucepan and warm over very low heat, stirring constantly. Pour into mug and garnish with a marshmallow.
Yield: 1 serving

Lime or Lemon Float

1½ c.	limeade or lemonade	375 mL
1 scoop	vanilla or fruit-flavored ice cream (p. 100 to 101)	1 scoop
1 slice	orange or lime	1 slice

Pour limeade or lemonade into a tall glass. Add ice cream and garnish with slice of orange or lime.
Yield: 1 serving

Fake Milk Shake

½ c.	orange juice	125 mL
½ c.	milk substitute	125 mL
1	banana	1
3 to 6	ice cubes	3 to 6

Put all ingredients in a blender and whip until frothy. Serve at once.
Yield: 2 servings

Morning Nog

1 c.	orange or pineapple juice	250 mL
1	egg	1
1 T.	honey	15 mL
3 to 6	ice cubes	3 to 6

Combine all ingredients in a blender until frothy.
Yield: 1 serving

BREADS AND QUICK BREADS

Look for the following prepared milk-free bread and bakery products:

Bread

Authentic French, Italian, rye, pumpernickel, egg, and pita or Syrian bread; PEPPERIDGE FARM French bread, club rolls and patty shells; bagels; STELLA D'ORO plain breadsticks; KINERET kosher frozen challa dough; KREAMO bakery products; plain melba toast; plain RY-KRISP; hamburger and hot dog buns purchased from a kosher bakery

Crackers

NABISCO Premium Saltine Crackers, Ritz Crackers, Wheatsworth Stone Ground Wheat Crackers, Uneeda Biscuit, Waverly Wafers, Triscuit Whole Wheat Wafers; ZESTA Saltine Crackers; KEEBLER Town House Oval Crackers

Other

AUNT JEMIMA Original Pancake and Waffle Mix (mix with water, milk substitute or fruit juice); MANISCHEWITZ "Some Stuff" Stuffing Mix; KELLOGG'S Corn Flake Crumbs.

Many additional locally made milk-free products can be found in the grocery store.

Breads and pancakes are usually made with milk, which acts as a softening agent and a sweetener. For yeast breads, milk is used to help the yeast grow. In this chapter, fruit juice, milk substitute and water have been substituted in recipes for bread leavened with baking powder or soda. In the yeast dough recipes, ginger ale has been used.

Milk-free bread crumbs are a boon to the cook who cannot use milk products in her recipes. Just one of their uses is as a substitute for grated Parmesan or other cheese that is sprinkled on top of a dish.

Garlic Bread

1 t	garlic salt, **or**	5 mL
½ t.	garlic powder, **or**	3 mL
2 cloves	garlic (crushed)	2 cloves
¼ c.	melted milk-free margarine	60 mL
1 large loaf	milk-free French bread	1 large loaf

In a small skillet, add garlic to melted margarine. Cut bread lengthwise into 2 pieces and spread with garlic "butter" mixture. Place under the broiler for 5 watchful minutes.
Yield: 1 loaf

VARIATION: Sauté one small onion in the margarine-and-garlic mixture. Sprinkle mixture with paprika. Follow other steps as before.

Pull-Apart Onion Bread

1 large loaf	milk-free French or Italian bread	1 large loaf
1 small	onion (minced)	1 small
½ c.	milk-free margarine	125 mL
½ t.	paprika	3 mL

Cut diagonal slices into but not through the bread at 2-in (5-cm) intervals. Sauté onion in margarine over very low heat. Sprinkle paprika onto onion. Spoon about 1 T. (15 mL) of onion mixture into each diagonal cut in the bread. Wrap entire loaf in foil. Place in oven and heat at 350 °F (175 °C) for 15 minutes.
Yield: 1 loaf

Milk-Free Bread Crumbs

Keep a plastic bag of milk-free bread crusts, ends, leftover rolls and other odd pieces of bread in the freezer. When you have accumulated a healthy amount, transfer the bread to a large bowl. Let the pieces of bread sit at room temperature uncovered for several days. When all the bread is hard, put it through a blender, food processor, electric grater or meat grinder. Store the crumbs in a covered container.

Bread crumbs taste best when a variety of breads and rolls are used together. Add herbs or spices if you wish. Refrigerate for longer shelf life.

Orange Nut Bread

1½ c.	flour	375 mL
½ c.	sugar	125 mL
2 t.	baking powder	10 mL
½ t.	salt	3 mL
¼ c.	melted milk-free margarine	60 mL
2	eggs	2
½ c.	orange juice	125 mL
¼ c.	nuts, chopped	60 mL

Combine flour, sugar, baking powder and salt. In a small bowl, combine the margarine, eggs and orange juice, and add to the dry ingredients. Mix well and pour into a greased 1 qt. (1 L) loaf pan. Let mixture sit at room temperature for 15 minutes. Sprinkle nuts on top. Bake at 325 °F (165 °C) 1 hour or until toothpick inserted in center comes out clean.
Yield: 1 loaf

Croutons

¼ c.	milk-free margarine	60 mL
½ t.	garlic salt	3 mL
2 c. ½-in. cubes	French or Italian bread	500 mL 1-cm cubes

Melt margarine in a small skillet and add garlic salt. Sauté bread cubes in margarine mixture, turning to brown all sides. These croutons may be stored at room temperature for several hours.
Yield: 2 c. (500 mL)

Mild Garlic Croutons

1 clove	garlic (minced)	1 clove
2 T.	vegetable oil	30 mL
1 c. ½-in. cubes	milk-free bread	250 mL 1-cm cubes

In a skillet, sauté garlic in oil. Add bread cubes, stirring to brown all sides. Remove to paper plate or paper towel.
Yield: 1 c. (250 mL)

Quick Pear Coffee Cake

¼ c.	salad oil	60 mL
1	egg (beaten)	1
½ c.	pear syrup (from can of pears)	125 mL
1½ c.	flour	375 mL
½ c.	sugar	125 mL
2 t.	baking powder	10 mL
½ t.	salt	3 mL
8-oz. can	pears	227 g
½ c.	flour	125 mL
¼ c.	brown sugar	60 mL

Combine oil, egg and pear syrup. Sift together flour, sugar, baking powder and salt. Add to egg mixture and beat well. Pour into a greased 9-in. (23-cm) square baking pan. Cover with sliced pears. Combine flour and brown sugar and sprinkle over pears; dot with margarine. Bake at 375 °F (190 °C) for about 25 minutes.
Yield: 9 servings

VARIATION: This cake can also be made with canned peaches or pineapple, and peach or pineapple syrup, in place of the pears and pear syrup. For more interest, add chopped maraschino cherries, nuts, chocolate chips, dried prunes or apricots. These ingredients can be chopped and tossed into the batter or sprinkled on top.

Crepes

3	eggs	3
1 t.	salt	5 mL
½ c.	water	125 mL
1½ c.	flour	375 mL
1 c.	water	250 mL
	milk-free margarine, melted	

Beat eggs, salt and ½ c. (125 mL) water with a wire whisk. Add flour and 1 c. (250 mL) water, and beat until thoroughly blended. Heat a 4-in. or 5-in. (9-cm or 12-cm) skillet on low flame and brush with enough melted milk-free margarine to grease pan bottom. Pour in about 2 T. (30 mL) batter and turn the pan so that the batter spreads over the entire bottom. Pour off excess. Cook on one side until the top is dry. Turn onto a paper towel. Continue this process until all the batter is gone. Crepes may be frozen.
Yield: 18 crepes

NOTE: For dessert crepes, gently turn and cook on the other side before removing from the skillet.

French Toast

2	eggs	2
¼ c.	milk substitute	60 mL
¼ c.	water	60 mL
6 slices	milk-free bread	6 slices
	milk-free margarine	

Beat eggs in a shallow bowl. Add milk substitute and water. Soak each slice of bread in egg mixture for 10 seconds on one side, turn and repeat. Cook both sides in a well-greased frying pan until golden.
Yield: 6 slices

VARIATION: For a different taste, use ½ c. (125 mL) orange or pineapple juice instead of water and milk substitute; ½ c. (125 mL) of water may also be used.

Pancakes

1 c.	flour	250 mL
1 T.	baking powder	15 mL
1 T.	sugar	15 mL
½ t.	salt	3 mL
1	egg (beaten)	1
½ c. each	orange juice and water	125 mL each
2 T.	vegetable oil	30 mL
	vegetable oil for griddle	

Mix together dry ingredients. Combine egg, orange juice mixture and oil. Add liquid to dry ingredients, stirring just until moist. Let mixture rest for 30 seconds. Spoon or pour batter onto greased hot griddle; cook pancakes on first side until bubbles appear on upper surface. Turn over and cook until bottom is golden.

Yield: About 12 large pancakes

Blueberry Muffins

1½ c.	flour	375 mL
½ c.	sugar	125 mL
2 t.	baking powder	10 mL
½ t.	salt	3 mL
1	egg (well-beaten)	1
½ c.	water	125 mL
⅓ c.	melted milk-free margarine	85 mL
1 c.	fresh blueberries	250 mL
	confectioners' sugar	

Grease one 12-cup muffin pan. Combine dry ingredients. In a small bowl, combine egg, water and margarine. Make a well in the center of the dry ingredients and add egg mixture all at once. Stir with a fork until just moist. Gently fold in blueberries. Fill muffin cups ⅔ full and bake at 400 °F (205 °C) for 25 to 30 minutes. Sprinkle tops with confectioners' sugar if desired.

Yield: 12 muffins

Banana Muffins

½ c.	milk-free margarine	125 mL
1 c.	sugar	250 mL
2	eggs	2
1 c.	mashed banana	250 mL
¾ t.	baking soda	180 mL
½ t.	salt	3 mL
1 c.	flour	250 mL

Grease one 12-cup muffin pan. Cream margarine and sugar. Add eggs, beating well, and stir in banana. Sift together dry ingredients. Add to banana mixture and mix well. Pour into greased muffin cups and bake at 350 °F (175 °C) for 25 to 30 minutes.
Yield: 12 muffins

NOTE: The mashed banana counts as the liquid in this recipe.

Refrigerator Rolls

1 pkg.	active dry yeast	1 pkg.
¼ c.	warm water	60 mL
1 c.	ginger ale	250 mL
¼ c.	sugar	60 mL
¼ c.	milk-free margarine	60 mL
1 t.	salt	5 mL
3½ c.	flour	875 mL
1	egg	1
¼ c.	melted milk-free margarine	60 mL

Soften yeast in the warm water and set aside; let cool to luke-warm. In a medium-size bowl combine ginger ale, sugar, margarine and salt. Add 1½ c. (375 mL) flour to this mixture and beat well. Beat in yeast and egg. Gradually add remaining flour, beating well. Place dough in a large greased bowl. Turn dough once to grease surface. Cover and chill overnight. Grease a 6-muffin pan. Form rolls by placing three 1-in. (2.5-cm) balls in each muffin cup and brush the top with melted margarine. Bake at 400 °F (200 °C) for 12 to 15 minutes.
Yield: 6 rolls

Cinnamon Rolls

1 pkg.	active dry yeast	1 pkg.
½ c.	warm water	125 mL
3 T.	sugar	45 mL
½ t.	salt	3 mL
2 T.	milk-free margarine (softened)	30 mL
1	egg	1
2 to 2½ c.	flour (unsifted)	500 to 625 mL
⅓ c.	melted milk-free margarine	85 mL
⅓ c.	sugar	85 mL
1 t.	cinnamon	5 mL
	Confectioners' Sugar Frosting (p. 92)	

Dissolve yeast in warm water. Beat in sugar, salt, margarine, egg and 1 c. (250 mL) flour. Add enough flour to make a soft dough. On a floured board, knead dough 2 minutes and roll out to 9 in. × 18 in. (23 cm × 45 cm). Brush with melted margarine; sprinkle with combined sugar and cinnamon. Roll up like a jelly roll. Seal sides firmly and cut into 12 equal pieces. Arrange on a greased 8-in. (20-cm) round pan. Cover with a damp cloth. Place covered rolls in a cold oven on a wire rack over a pan of boiling water. Let rolls rise 30 minutes. Uncover rolls, remove rack and pan of water. Turn oven to 375 °F (190 °C) and bake for 30 to 35 minutes. While rolls are warm, frost with Confectioners' Sugar Frosting.
Yield: 12 rolls

SALADS AND DRESSINGS

Salads are an important staple in the milk-free diet. They are rich in vitamins and minerals, loaded with fibre, and safely eaten at home, in a restaurant or at a friend's home. In general, most types of salad dressings are made without milk products. Any of the Italian or vinegar-and-oil dressings are milk-free, as are French, lemon juice, and mayonnaise dressings. Bottled dressings are widely available without milk but be sure to skip the cream or yogurt dressings. You can make creamy dressings at home with the recipes given in this chapter based on mayonnaise, mashed avocado or milk-free whipping cream.

Milk-free salad dressings are made by WISHBONE, REESE, KRAFT, WEIGHT WATCHERS, SEVEN SEAS, MARZETTI and PFEIFFER.

Vegetable Salads

Stuffed Tomato Salad

6	firm tomatoes	6
½ c.	cucumber, diced	125 mL
¼ c.	green pepper, diced	60 mL
¼ c.	celery, diced	60 mL
¼ c.	hearts of palm, diced	60 mL
	salt and pepper to taste	
2 T.	vinegar and oil dressing	30 mL
	dried dill	

Rinse and dry tomatoes; slice off tops and discard. Scoop out seeds and pulp; mix seeds and pulp with diced cucumber, green pepper, celery and hearts of palm. Add salt and pepper and dressing. Fill tomato cups with diced vegetable mixture and top with a sprinkle of dill.
Yield: 6 servings

Caesar Salad

1 head	romaine lettuce (washed and dried)	1 head
1 clove	garlic	1 clove
2-oz. can	boneless anchovies	57 g
¼ c.	salad oil	60 mL
¼ t.	salt	1.5 mL
dash	white pepper	dash
2 t.	Worcestershire sauce	10 mL
1 T.	lemon juice	15 mL
2	eggs (coddled)	2
	Mild Garlic Croutons (p. 40)	

Tear romaine leaves into large pieces and place in a wooden bowl that has been rubbed with garlic. Mash anchovies and combine with oil, salt, pepper, Worcestershire sauce and lemon juice. Blend well. Pour this on top of romaine leaves. Pour eggs over and toss with two forks. Add croutons and toss again. Serve at once.

Yield: 4–6 servings

Spinach Salad I

1 lb.	spinach (rinsed and dried, stems removed)	450 g
1 c.	water chestnuts	250 mL
11-oz. can	mandarin oranges (drained)	312 g
½ c.	oil	125 mL
½ c.	sugar	125 mL
½ c.	vinegar	125 mL
½ c.	chili sauce	125 mL
1 t.	salt	5 mL
1 small	onion, diced (optional)	1 small

Toss together spinach, water chestnuts and mandarin orange sections in a salad bowl. In a separate bowl, combine remaining ingredients to make dressing. Pour dressing over salad and serve.

Yield: 4 servings

Spinach Salad II

two 11-oz. cans	mandarin orange sections	two 312-g cans
1 lb.	spinach (rinsed, drained, stems removed)	450 g
1 medium	red onion (thinly sliced)	1 medium
1 c.	mayonnaise	250 mL
2 T.	honey	30 mL
1 T.	lemon juice	15 mL
¼ c.	sunflower seeds (unsalted)	60 mL

Drain mandarin oranges, retaining juice. Toss together spinach, onion slices and mandarin orange sections. Combine ¼ c. (60 mL) juice from mandarin oranges with mayonnaise, honey and lemon juice. Pour onto salad. Sprinkle salad with about 3 T. (45 mL) sunflower seeds and toss again. Garnish salad with remaining sunflower seeds.
Yield: 4 servings

Four-Bean Salad

16-oz. can	green beans	454 g
16-oz. can	waxed beans	454 g
16-oz. can	garbanzo beans	454 g
16-oz. can	kidney beans	454 g
½ c.	onion, chopped	125 mL
½ c.	green pepper, minced	125 mL
½ c.	vegetable oil	125 mL
½ c.	vinegar	125mL
¾ c.	sugar	185 mL
1 t.	salt	5 mL
½ t.	white pepper	3 mL
¼ t.	prepared mustard	1.5 mL

Empty cans of beans into a colander and rinse and drain well. Remove loose skins from garbanzo beans; place beans in a bowl and add onion and green pepper. To make dressing, mix remaining ingredients, stirring well to dissolve sugar. Pour dressing over beans and refrigerate for several hours before serving. Mix occasionally.
Yield: 4–6 servings

Potato Salad

12	baking potatoes	12
2	eggs (hard-boiled and chopped)	2
1 t.	prepared mustard	5 mL
¼ c.	chives, chopped	60 mL
¼ c.	green pepper, chopped	60 mL
¼ c.	celery, chopped	60 mL
¼ c.	mayonnaise	60 mL
	salt to taste	

The night before, boil potatoes in skins until soft; refrigerate potatoes. The next day, peel jackets off cold potatoes and cut potatoes into large chunks. Add chopped egg, mustard, chives, green pepper and celery and toss. Mix in mayonnaise, starting with ¼ c. (60 mL) and adding more if necessary; add salt. Refrigerate thoroughly before serving.
Yield: 8–12 servings

Sweet and Saucy Cucumbers

½ c.	water	125 mL
½ c.	vinegar	125 mL
3 T.	sugar	45 mL
2 medium	cucumbers (peeled, sliced thin)	2 medium

Mix water, vinegar and sugar. Pour over sliced cucumbers and refrigerate for at least 24 hours.
Yield: 4 servings

Vegetable Salad Toppers

Basic Mayonnaise Dressing

Mix together equal parts of mayonnaise and ketchup.

VARIATIONS: Add chili sauce, beets and beet juice, white horseradish, spinach juice or your favorite preserves to the mayonnaise-ketchup mixture. Always be sure to use real mayonnaise to which dry milk has not been added.

Thousand Island Dressing

½ c.	mayonnaise	125 mL
½ c.	ketchup	125 mL
2 T.	sweet pickle relish	30 mL
1	egg, hard-boiled and chopped (optional)	1

Combine ingredients, mix and refrigerate.
Yield: About 1½ c. (375 mL)

Avocado Dressing

2 medium	avocados (mashed)	2 medium
1 T.	lemon juice	15 mL
1 small	onion (minced)	1 small
½ c.	mayonnaise	125 mL

Combine ingredients, mix and refrigerate.
Yield: About 1 c. (250 mL)

Italian Dressing

1 c.	salad oil	250 mL
¼ c.	vinegar	60 mL
1 t.	sugar	5 mL
½ t.	salt	3 mL
¼ t.	white pepper	1.5 mL
¼ t.	celery seed	1.5 mL
1 clove	garlic (minced)	1 clove

Combine ingredients, mix and refrigerate. Shake well before serving.
Yield: About 1½ c. (375 mL)

Sour Creamless Green Goddess Dressing

2 c.	mayonnaise	500 mL
2 T.	chives, chopped	30 mL
1 T.	parsley flakes	15 mL
8	anchovy fillets (finely chopped)	8
2 t.	lemon juice	10 mL

Combine ingredients, mix and refrigerate.
Yield: About 2 c. (500 mL)

Fruit Salads

Milk-free fruit products include fruit sauces like apple, plum or cranberry. Your local dairy or delicatessen might carry fruit salads prepared without milk products. It is always better to speak with the counterperson about the ingredients used in prepared salads rather than guess about them. When in doubt about a salad, pass it up.

Old-Fashioned Waldorf Salad

3 c.	apple chunks	750 mL
½ c.	walnuts, chopped	125 mL
½ c.	celery, chopped	125 mL
½ c.	raisins	125 mL
1 to 2 T.	mayonnaise	15 to 30 mL

Blend ingredients, using enough mayonnaise to moisten. Refrigerate, covered, for about an hour before serving.
Yield: 4–6 servings

Autumn Fruit Salad

2	soft pears (peeled	2
or	and diced	**or**
8-oz. can	sliced pears (drained)	227 g
2	firm bananas (sliced)	2
2	ripe apples (skinned, cored, and cut into chunks)	2
2	navel oranges (peeled and sectioned)	2
1	pink or yellow grapefruit (peeled and sectioned)	1
1 to 2 T.	mayonnaise	15 to 30 mL

Gently toss the fruit in a chilled bowl. Add enough mayonnaise to moisten. Serve immediately.
Yield: 4–6 servings

Summer Fruit Salad

2 c.	watermelon balls	500 mL
1 c.	cantaloupe balls	250 mL
1 c.	honeydew balls	250 mL
1 pt.	fresh blueberries (rinsed and drained)	500 mL
2 t.	sugar	10 mL

Put fruit in a bowl and sprinkle with sugar. Cover bowl and refrigerate for 1 to 2 hours. Some liquid will fill the bottom of the bowl; toss fruit with liquid immediately before serving.
Yield: 4–6 servings

Ambrosia

2 to 3	oranges (peeled and sectioned)	2 to 3
2	firm bananas (sliced)	2
1 c.	canned pineapple chunks (drained)	250 mL
1 c.	miniature marshmallows	250 mL
½ c.	maraschino cherries	125 mL
¼ c.	sugar	60 mL
¼ c.	cherry juice	60 mL
	shredded coconut	

Gently toss oranges, bananas, pineapple, marshmallows and cherries. Sprinkle on sugar and cherry juice. Add desired amount of coconut and toss again. Chill thoroughly.
Yield: 4–6 servings

Fruit Salad Toppers

Strawberry Dressing

1 c.	hulled strawberries	250 mL
½ c.	confectioners' sugar	125 mL
1	egg white	1

Mash strawberries in a bowl. Add sugar and mix. In a separate bowl, beat egg white until stiff. Add egg white to strawberry mixture, beating well. Spoon onto any fruit salad.
Yield: About 1 c. (250 mL)

Whipped Topping Dressing

8-oz. container	milk-free whipping cream	227 g
½ c.	chopped walnuts	125 mL

Mix whipping cream according to directions. Add nuts and spoon onto fruit salad or slices.
Yield: 2 c. (500mL)

Gelatin Salads

Salads based on unflavored or flavored gelatin are welcome accompaniments any time of year and can be served before, during or after a meal. Gelatin salads are safely eaten in restaurants provided the gelatin is clear and cream-free. At home, prepare clear gelatin or creamy gelatin, using mayonnaise or milk-free whipping cream as a sour cream or cream cheese substitute. Remember that when you base a recipe on unflavored gelatin, you should use the required amount of water or fruit juice when adding other ingredients like fruit. If you begin with a flavored gelatin, reduce the amount of liquid by about a third when adding fruit or slivered vegetables. If the recipe calls for 2 c. (500 mL) of boiling water (and it must be boiling), reduce the amount to 1 ⅓ c. (335 mL) water.

Citrus Mould

3-oz. pkg.	orange gelatin	85 g
3-oz. pkg.	raspberry gelatin	85 g
1⅔ c.	hot orange juice	420 mL
1⅔ c.	cold grapefruit juice	420 mL
1½ c.	milk-free whipped cream	375 mL
2	navel oranges (sectioned)	2
1	grapefruit (sectioned)	1

In a bowl, mix orange and raspberry gelatin crystals. Add hot orange juice and stir until dissolved. Add grapefruit juice and let mixture sit at room temperature. When thick, but not set, beat in whipped cream until well-blended. Line bottom of a 6-cup (1.5-L) circular mould alternately with orange and grapefruit sections. Fill with gelatin mixture and chill until firm; fruit will rise.
Yield: 6–8 servings

Cherry Waldorf Gelatin

3-oz. pkg.	apple gelatin	85 g
1 c.	boiling water	250 mL
1 c.	cold water	250 mL
3-oz. pkg.	cherry gelatin	85 g
⅔ c.	boiling water	170 mL
⅔ c.	cold water	170 mL
1½ t.	lemon juice	8 mL
½ c.	mayonnaise	125 mL
½ c.	apples, chopped	125 mL
½ c.	walnuts, chopped	125 mL
dollop	mayonnaise	dollop

Dissolve apple gelatin in 1 c. (250 mL) boiling water. Add 1 c. (250 mL) cold water and stir. Pour into a 3-c. (750-mL) mould and refrigerate. Prepare cherry gelatin by dissolving in ⅔ c. (170 mL) boiling water and adding ⅔ c. (170 mL) cold water; add lemon juice. Refrigerate cherry gelatin until thick and syrupy, then beat in mayonnaise and fold in apples and walnuts. Set aside. When apple gelatin is almost set, pour cherry mixture on top. Chill until firm. Unmould gelatin onto a serving plate and garnish with a dollop of mayonnaise.
Yield: 6 to 8 servings

Carrot-Orange-Banana Moulds

1 T.	unflavored gelatin	15 mL
¼ c.	cold water	60 mL
1 c.	hot orange juice	250 mL
½ c.	sugar	125 mL
½ c.	bananas, sliced	125 mL
½ c.	orange sections, diced	125 mL
¼ c.	carrot, shredded	60 mL

Soften gelatin in the cold water. Add hot orange juice and stir until gelatin is dissolved; stir in sugar. Chill until syrupy, then fold in bananas, oranges and carrots. Pour into four individual ½-c. (125-mL) moulds and chill until firm.
Yield: 4 servings

Birthday Party Treats

¾ c.	miniature marshmallows	
	(white or tinted)	185 mL
⅔ c.	boiling water	170 mL
3-oz. pkg.	lime or other	85 g
	flavored gelatin	
⅔ c.	cold water	170 mL
½ c.	milk-free	125 mL
	whipped cream	
6	paper baking cups	6

Spray a standard 6-cup muffin tin with nonstick vegetable spray. Place about 8 miniature marshmallows in each section. In a medium-size bowl, add boiling water to the gelatin, stirring until dissolved. Add the cold water and blend well. Pour 2 T. (30 mL) gelatin over marshmallows in each muffin cup. Chill until very thick. Meanwhile, let the rest of the gelatin set at room temperature; when thick, but not set, add whipped cream and beat well. Fill each marshmallow cup with gelatin/whipped cream mixture and chill until firm. Flatten the paper baking cups and use one as a doily under each marshmallow cup; unmould and serve.

Yield: 6 servings

MAIN DISHES

With the exception of creamed foods, milk itself is not called for in main dishes as it is in baking or breadmaking. Cheese, however, is another story. I rely heavily on the combination of egg and bread crumbs as a cheese substitute.

Tofu, a soy bean product resembling the consistency of cheese, can also be used. Tofu is rich in protein and has the versatility of cheese. It can be sliced and used in sandwiches. It can also be crumbled and tossed in salads, whipped for salad dressings, cubed, stir-fried, baked or broiled. Tofu takes on the taste of the foods or spices with which it is mixed. It does not, however, melt like cheese.

Creamed dishes can be made with bouillon- or ketchup-based sauces. Another objective of these main-dish recipes is to provide an alternative to fried foods. In order to get the highest vitamin content possible, I have exchanged baking for frying in several recipes. The taste difference is minimal, while the digestibility difference is great.

Order simply prepared main dishes when eating in a restaurant. Be sure to have the chef omit the butter or margarine from the preparation. Enjoy grilled steaks or chops, broiled chicken, baked or broiled fish, roast turkey or beef. If you order your dish prepared with no breading, sauces or gravies, you'll be safe.

Meat

When selecting meat, choose only true and basic cuts. Buy hamburger that is composed entirely of ground sirloin, round or chuck. Forget the processed meats as a rule, but you may select kosher products such as bologna, salami, corned beef, pastrami and beef sausages. If the product bears a kosher label, it is free of milk and milk by-products. BEST kosher meats, FEINBERG kosher meats, HEBREW NATIONAL kosher meats, EMPIRE frozen dinners and MA COHEN'S frozen dinners are examples of brands to look for.

Lasagne

4 c.	Spaghetti Sauce (p. 83)	1 L
16-oz. box	lasagne	454 g
2 c.	Milk-Free Bread Crumbs (p. 38–39)	500 mL

Bring spaghetti sauce to a boil, then remove from heat and set aside. In a large pot, cook lasagne according to instructions on box. Line a 9 × 13-in. (23 × 33-cm) square glass baking dish or large lasagne pan with half of the lasagne and spread half of the sauce over the lasagne. Top with half of the bread crumbs. Layer on remaining lasagne, sauce and bread crumbs. Cover with aluminum foil; bake at 350 °F (175 °C) for 30 minutes. Uncover and continue baking for an additional 30 minutes.
Yield: 6–8 servings

NOTE: If you can tolerate a small amount of cottage cheese, add this between the layers of meat sauce and bread crumbs. Tofu may be added in place of the cheese.

Oven-Baked Pork Ribs

2 to 3 lbs.	pork ribs	900 g to 1.4 kg
	salt	
	pepper	
	celery seed	to taste
	barbecue sauce	

Preheat oven to 450 °F (230 °C). Place ribs in a shallow pan and sear in the oven for 30 minutes; pour off fat. Turn over and sear for another 30 minutes; pour off fat. Season with salt, pepper and celery seed and bake for 30 minutes at 350 °F (175 °C). Top with barbecue sauce and bake an additional 15 minutes.
Yield: 4 servings

Beef Burgundy

1 small	onion (sliced)	1 small
2 T	milk-free margarine	30 mL
2 to 3 lbs.	chuck (cut into small pieces)	900 g to 1.4 kg
1 T.	flour	15 mL
1 t.	salt	5 mL
¼ t.	white pepper	1.5 mL
2 c.	beef broth	500 mL
1 c.	Burgundy wine	250 mL
1 lb.	fresh mushrooms	450 g

Sauté onion in margarine; add meat and brown. Add flour, salt and pepper and stir until smooth. Add ½ c. (125 mL) broth and ¾ c. (250 mL) wine. Simmer 3 hours. Add mushrooms and simmer another hour. When mixture needs more liquid, add remaining wine or broth.
Yield: 8 servings

Pepper Steak

2 T.	vegetable oil	30 mL
1 small	onion (sliced)	1 small
1 to 2 lbs.	round chuck steak, cut into ¼-in. (6-mm) strips	450 to 900 g
2 large	green peppers (seeded, cut into chunks)	2 large
3	tomatoes (cut into wedges)	3
1 T.	soy sauce	15 mL
2 T.	Worcestershire sauce	30 mL

Heat oil in large skillet and lightly brown onion. Add meat strips and brown on both sides. Add peppers, tomatoes, soy sauce and Worcestershire sauce. Bring to a boil. Cover and simmer 1 hour, or until meat is very tender.
Yield: 4–6 servings

Hamburgers

1 lb.	ground beef **or**	450 g
½ lb. each	beef and veal	225 g each
1	egg	1
½ c.	Milk-Free Bread Crumbs (p. 38–39)	125 mL
¼ c.	milk substitute or ketchup	60 mL
1 t.	Worcestershire sauce	5 mL
	salt and pepper to taste	

Mix all ingredients and blend well. Form 4 hamburgers and broil, bake or grill.
Yield: 4 servings

"Who Needs Cheese!" Toppers

Cheese isn't the only way to dress up a hamburger. Try one of these:

Grilled tomato	Italian sausages
Pineapple slices	Barbecue sauce
Spaghetti sauce with extra oregano	Bacon slices

    Mixture of ½ ketchup, ½ mayonnaise, and pickle relish to taste

Oven Meatballs

1 c.	Milk-Free Bread Crumbs (p. 38–39)	250 mL
2	eggs	2
½ c.	water	125 mL
1 T.	ketchup	15 mL
1 T.	onion, minced	15 mL
2 t.	salt	10 mL
½ t.	white pepper	3 mL
½ t.	paprika	3 mL
1½ lbs.	ground beef	675 g

Put bread crumbs in a bowl. Add eggs and water and beat slightly with a fork. Season with ketchup, onion, salt, pepper and paprika. Add meat and blend well. Roll into 2-in. (5-cm) balls. Bake in a shallow baking pan for 30 minutes at 350 °F (175 °C).
Yield: 6–8 servings

Sweet and Sour Meatballs

1 lb.	ground beef or veal	450 g
1	egg	1
½ c.	Milk-Free Bread Crumbs (p. 38–39)	125 mL
1½ T.	salt	25 mL
2 t.	garlic salt	10 mL
1 t.	white pepper	5 mL
1½ c.	ketchup	375 mL
2 T.	milk substitute	30 mL
1 c.	ginger ale	250 mL
½ c.	grape jelly	125 mL

In a bowl combine the meat, egg, bread crumbs, salt, garlic salt and pepper. Add ½ c. (125 mL) ketchup and milk substitute; blend well. In a saucepan, pour remaining ketchup, ginger ale and jelly. Stir over low heat until mixture just boils. With wet hands, form 1-in. (2.5-cm) meatballs and drop into cooking sauce. Cover and simmer for 1 hour.
Yield: 4–6 servings

Ground Veal in Acorn Squash

1 lb.	ground veal	450 g
1	egg	1
2 T.	Milk-Free Bread Crumbs (p. 38–39)	30 mL
½ c.	green pepper, chopped	125 mL
1 T.	onion, minced	15 mL
	salt and pepper to taste	
3	acorn squash	3
2 large	tomatoes (sliced)	2 large

In a bowl, blend veal, egg, bread crumbs, green pepper and onion. Add salt and pepper. Cut squash in half and scoop out the seeds. Fill each half with meat mixture and top with a tomato slice; sprinkle with bread crumbs. Arrange on a cookie sheet and cover each squash half with aluminum foil. Bake at 350 °F (175 °C) for 30 minutes. Uncover and continue baking another 15 minutes, or until squash is soft.
Yield: 6 servings

Italian Veal

2 T.	vegetable oil	30 mL
1 clove	garlic (minced)	1 clove
½ c.	onion, minced	125 mL
1 lb.	veal (sliced thin)	450 g
2 c.	tomato sauce	500 mL
1 t.	salt	5 mL
1 t.	oregano	5 mL
¼ t.	white pepper	1.5 mL

Heat oil in skillet and sauté garlic and onion; remove and set aside. Sauté veal on both sides until browned. Add tomato sauce, salt, oregano, white pepper, onion and garlic and simmer for about 30 minutes. Serve over noodles.
Yield: 4 servings

Veal Tidbits

½ lb.	sliced mushrooms	225 g
2 T.	vegetable oil	30 mL
1 lb.	veal shoulder (sliced thin)	450 g
	salt	
	white pepper } to taste	
	garlic salt	
½ c.	white wine	125 mL
2 T.	water	30 mL

Sauté mushrooms in 1 T. (15 mL) oil; set aside. In another T. (15 mL) oil, sauté veal gently on each side. Line a baking dish with veal and season with salt, pepper and garlic salt. Spread mushrooms on top. Pour in white wine and water. Bake at 350 °F (175 °C) for 45 minutes. If veal becomes dry during baking, add a little water.
Yield: 4 servings

Poultry

Buy only fresh or frozen poultry that is free of additives and automatic basting butters. Rely on homemade turkey breast rather than store-bought turkey or chicken rolls. Pass over the frozen breaded poultry in general, though you can select kosher-pareve prepared fried chicken. EMPIRE, MANIS-CHEWITZ and MA COHEN'S are national brands that make prepared milk-free poultry products.

Cold Chicken and Pasta

4 to 5	whole chicken breasts (boned)	4 to 5
	water	
	chicken bouillon	
16-oz. box	vermicelli	454 g
2 T.	white wine vinegar	30 mL
2 cloves	garlic (crushed)	2 cloves
½ c.	olive oil	125 mL
two 8.5-oz. jars	artichoke hearts	two 241-g jars
6-oz. can	black olives (pitted)	168 g
½ lb.	cherry tomatoes	225 g
1 c.	mayonnaise	250 mL
2 t.	Dijon mustard	10 mL
2 t.	salt	10 mL

Place chicken breasts in large pot and add a mixture of half water, half bouillon, enough to cover chicken. Bring to boil and cook for 30 minutes; pour off broth. Cool, skin and cube the chicken, then cover and refrigerate. Cook vermicelli according to directions on box; drain and set aside. Mix together vinegar, garlic, oil and salt. Toss vermicelli with this mixture and chill thoroughly. Drain artichoke hearts and olives; slice olives. Rinse tomatoes and remove stems. Add the chicken cubes to the vermicelli and blend in mayonnaise and mustard. Add olives and artichokes to the chicken-and-pasta mixture. Garnish with cherry tomatoes.
Yield: 8 servings

Oven-Fried Chicken

2 to 3 lbs.	fryer chicken (cut up)	900 g-1.4 kg
2 c.	Milk-Free Bread Crumbs (p. 38–39)	500 mL
½ t.	garlic salt	3 mL
1 t.	salt	5 mL
½ t.	white pepper	3 mL
	milk-free margarine	

Rinse chicken in cold water. *Do not dry.* Roll in bread crumbs. Place in a baking pan. Mix spices together and shake evenly over chicken. Dot each piece with margarine. Bake uncovered, without turning, at 375 °F (190 °C) for about 1 hour.
Yield: 4 servings

Broiled Chicken

2 to 3 lbs.	broiler or fryer chicken (rinsed, dried, and cut up)	900 g-1.4 kg
½ c.	soy sauce	125 mL
¼ c.	Worcestershire sauce	60 mL
2 pinches	crushed rosemary	2 pinches

Put chicken pieces top down in broiler pan, leaving some room around each; don't overcrowd. In a small bowl, mix together soy sauce and Worcestershire sauce and add rosemary. Drizzle half the sauce over chicken and broil. Turn pieces over and drizzle remainder of sauce on the other side. Total broiling time is about 40 minutes.
Yield: 4 servings

Chicken Divan

10-oz. pkg	frozen broccoli **or**	283 g
½ lb.	fresh broccoli	450 g
	Chicken Sauce (p. 65)	
8 slices	chicken breast (cooked)	8 slices
	Milk-Free Bread Crumbs (p. 38–39)	

Steam broccoli. Prepare Chicken Sauce. Arrange broccoli in an 8 × 11-in. (20 × 28-cm) casserole dish and pour half of the

Chicken Sauce over it. Cover with chicken slices. Pour remaining sauce over chicken and top with a heavy sprinkling of bread crumbs. Bake uncovered at 375 °F (190 °C) for 30 minutes.
Yield: 4 servings

Chicken à l'Orange

1	egg (slightly beaten)	1
¼ c.	orange juice	60 mL
1 c.	Milk-Free Bread Crumbs (p. 38–39)	250 mL
1 t.	paprika	5 mL
1 t.	salt	5 mL
1 T.	orange peel, grated	15 mL
2 to 3 lbs.	fryer chicken	900 g-1.4 kg
	(rinsed, dried, and cut up)	

Combine egg and orange juice; beat. Combine bread crumbs, paprika, salt and orange peel. Dip chicken in egg mixture, then into bread-crumb mixture. Bake covered at 375 °F (190 °C) for 30 minutes. Uncover and bake another 15 minutes.
Yield: 4 servings

Chicken Sauce

2 T.	milk-free margarine	30 mL
2 T.	flour	30 mL
2 c.	chicken bouillon	500 mL
	salt and white pepper to taste	
1	egg yolk	1
2 T.	sherry	30 mL

Melt margarine in a saucepan and add flour. Blend well. Slowly pour in 1½ c. (375 mL) bouillon. Add salt and pepper, stirring constantly. When mixture boils, blend 2 T. (30 mL) of hot sauce with egg yolk. Add egg mixture to hot sauce and stir constantly until well blended. Add sherry and cook on low heat, stirring constantly for 10 minutes. Add more sherry or bouillon if necessary.
Yield: 2 c. (500 mL)

Turkey à la King

2 c.	turkey (cooked and diced)	500 mL
3-oz. can	sliced mushrooms	85 g
½ c.	green pepper, chopped	125 mL
½ c.	frozen or fresh peas (cooked)	125 mL
¼ c.	pimiento, chopped	60 mL
	White Sauce I (p. 81)	

Combine all ingredients and simmer for 20 to 30 minutes, stirring occasionally. To serve, pour over toast points or into patty shells.
Yield: 4–6 servings

Turkey-Grape-Cashew Salad

3 c.	turkey (cooked and diced)	750 mL
½ lb.	cashew nuts (salted)	225 mL
1 lb.	green grapes (seedless)	450 g
	mayonnaise ⎱ to taste	
	salt and pepper ⎰	
	lettuce	

Toss turkey, cashews and grapes together with enough mayonnaise to make a creamy consistency. Season with salt and pepper if desired. Serve on a bed of lettuce.
Yield: 4–6 servings

NOTE: Hot garlic bread or soup makes a good accompaniment to this salad.

Fish and Seafood

Fresh, frozen and canned fish and shellfish can be used in milk-free recipes, but avoid breaded and creamed seafood products. If you must purchase prepared fish dishes, only kosher-pareve products can safely be assumed to be milk-free.

Baked Fillet of Flounder

1	flounder fillet	1
½ t.	mayonnaise	3 mL
1 T.	Milk-Free Bread Crumbs (p. 38–39)	15 mL
	milk-free margarine	
	salt (optional)	
1 T.	lemon juice	15 mL

Rinse the fillet and lay it flat in a greased baking dish. Pour lemon juice over fish. Spread ½ t. (3 mL) mayonnaise on top, sprinkle with bread crumbs and dot with margarine. Sprinkle with salt if desired. Bake uncovered at 350 °F (175 °C) for 40 minutes or until bread crumbs are toasty.
Yield: 1 serving

Oven-Fried Scallops

½ lb.	scallops	225 g
¾ c.	Milk-Free Bread Crumbs (p. 38–39)	185 mL
½ t.	salt	3 mL
¼ t.	white pepper	1.5 mL
¼ t.	paprika	1.5 mL
2	eggs (beaten)	2

Rinse scallops in cold water. Mix together bread crumbs, salt, pepper and paprika. Dip each scallop in egg and then roll in bread-crumb mixture. Place scallops on an oiled cookie sheet and bake at 450 °F (230 °C) for about 12 to 15 minutes. Scallops should be crisp on the outside and soft on the inside.
Yield: 1 serving

Shrimp in Pita

1	avocado (mashed)	1
2 t.	chives, chopped	10 mL
1 t.	lime or lemon juice	5 mL
⅓ c.	cucumber, chopped	85 mL
1 T.	mayonnaise	15 mL
	salt and pepper to taste	
1 c.	shrimp (cooked and diced)	250 mL
2 small	rounds of pita bread	2 small

In a small bowl, mix avocado, chives, lime juice and cucumber. Add mayonnaise and blend well. Add salt and pepper. Gently blend in shrimp. Heat pita bread in oven set at 350 °F (175 °C) for 10 minutes. Cut each pita round in half and stuff pockets with shrimp mixture.
Yield: 4 sandwiches

Shrimp de Jonghe

½ c.	milk-free margarine	125 mL
1 clove	garlic (chopped fine)	1 clove
¼ c.	parsley flakes	60 mL
½ t.	paprika	3 mL
¼ t.	white pepper	1.5 mL
½ c.	dry white wine	125 mL
1½ c.	Milk-Free Bread Crumbs (p. 38–39)	375 mL
4 c.	shrimp (cooked)	1 L

In a small saucepan, on very low heat, melt margarine and add garlic, parsley flakes, paprika and pepper. Slowly stir in wine and blend well. Pour bread crumbs in a medium-size bowl, add margarine mixture and mix well. Spread shrimp in a 9-in. (23-cm) square baking dish. Cover with bread-crumb mixture. Bake at 350 °F (175 °C) for 25 minutes, or until well browned.
Yield: 6 servings

Stuffed Fillet of Sole

½ c.	milk-free margarine	125 mL
¼ c.	onion, chopped	60 mL
¼ c.	almonds (blanched and finely chopped)	60 mL
½ c.	shallots or green onion, chopped	125 mL
¼ c.	tomato, chopped	60 mL
8	sole fillets (fresh or frozen)	8
2 T.	lemon juice	30 mL
	Milk-Free Bread Crumbs (p. 38–39)	
	milk-free margarine	

Melt margarine in a frying pan and sauté the onion, almonds, shallots and tomato for 1 minute; set aside. Rinse the fillets in cold water; roll loosely and stand each fillet upright in a cup of a muffin tin. Fill the fillets with the nut mixture, pour on a little lemon juice, sprinkle with bread crumbs and dot with margarine. Bake fillets in the muffin tin at 375 °F (190 °C) for about 30 minutes.

Yield: 4 servings

Eggs

Many standard egg recipes, such as omelets and scrambled eggs, include milk or cream. Water, or a combination of half milk substitute and half water, works well. Try fruit juice for a different taste. Remember that fresh eggs yield a frothier consistency when beaten than do stale eggs. To test for freshness, hold the egg next to your ear and gently shake it. If the egg glides gently from side to side, it is fresh. If you can hear the egg hit the sides of the shell, it is stale.

Deviled Eggs

6	eggs (hard-boiled)	6
2 T.	pickle relish	30 mL
1 T.	mayonnaise	15 mL
1 T.	prepared mustard	15 mL
½ t.	Worcestershire sauce	3 mL
¼ t.	salt	1.5 mL
	paprika	

Cut eggs in half lengthwise and remove yolks. Add remaining ingredients to yolks and blend until smooth. Refill egg whites and sprinkle with paprika.
Yield: 12 deviled eggs

Eggs Benedict

4 slices	grilled ham	4 slices
4 slices	milk-free toast	4 slices
4	eggs (poached)	4
	Hollandaise Sauce (p. 82)	

Place a slice of ham over each piece of toast. Top with a poached egg and pour on Hollandaise Sauce.
Yield: 4 servings

NOTE: To poach an egg, bring 3 in. (7.5 cm) of water to a boil in a saucepan, then turn the heat to low. Stir the water to create a well in the center and slip the egg into the well. Cook the egg for 3 to 5 minutes, depending on your preference for doneness. Remove the egg with a slotted spoon.

Company Scrambled Eggs

12	eggs	12
½ c.	water	125 mL
¼ c.	milk substitute	60 mL
½ t.	salt	3 mL
¼ t.	white pepper	1.5 mL
¼ t .	dill	1.5 mL
¼ t.	oregano	1.5 mL
3 T.	milk-free margarine	45 mL

Beat eggs with a wire whisk. Add all other ingredients except margarine and beat again until very frothy. Melt margarine in a large frying pan and cook eggs over low heat, turning occasionally. Remove when fully cooked, yet still moist.
Yield: 6 servings

NOTE: Serve with sautéed chicken livers, sautéed onions or sautéed green pepper.

Spanish Omelet

6	eggs (separated)	6
⅓ c.	water	85 mL
½ t.	salt	3 mL
3 T.	milk-free margarine	45 mL
¼ c.	green pepper, chopped	60 mL
¼ c.	tomato, chopped	60 mL
1 T.	onion, minced	15 mL

Beat the egg whites until bubbly; add water and salt and beat until thick. In a separate bowl, beat the yolks until very thick and lemon-colored. Fold yolks into whites. Melt half the margarine in a frying pan; when a drop of water sizzles in the pan, pour in half of the egg mixture. Reduce heat and cook until bottom is browned. Add half of the vegetables, and fold omelet over and finish cooking on both sides. Remove omelet from pan and repeat the process with the remaining ingredients.
Yield: 2 servings

VEGETABLES, SOUPS AND SAUCES

Vegetables

All fresh, frozen and canned vegetables are safe to eat provided they are plain. LA CHOY Oriental vegetable and sauce mixes are a good choice for something different. Skip over vegetables prepared in butter sauce or cream sauce. Vegetables prepared "Hawaiian style" or "New England style," etc., are best passed over unless you make them at home in individual bags and freeze. Consider investing in an electric bag sealer. The bags are boilable and make "home-style" just as convenient as store-bought vegetables.

Squash and Pear Bake

1 large	butternut squash	1 large
8-oz. can	pear halves	227 g
½ c.	brown sugar	125 mL
2 T.	milk-free margarine	30 mL

Bake whole squash at 375 °F (190 °C) for about 45 minutes, until softened yet still somewhat firm. If using a microwave, slash squash with a knife; otherwise, squash could burst. Remove skin and slice into ½-in. (1-cm) pieces, discarding seeds. Grease a glass baking dish. Place in the dish, alternately, one piece of squash and one pear half until dish is full. Sprinkle with brown sugar and dot with margarine. Bake at 325 °F (165 °C) for 30 minutes, or until squash is completely soft and mixture is slightly browned.
Yield: 4–6 servings

Ratatouille

3 T.	vegetable oil	45 mL
3 small	onions (peeled and chopped)	3 small
1 small	green pepper (seeded and cut into strips)	1 small
½ small	eggplant (peeled, sliced, and cut into strips)	½ small
1 small	zucchini (peeled and cut into strips)	1 small
2 small	tomatoes (cut into wedges)	2 small
1 lb.	fresh mushrooms	450 g
	salt and pepper to taste	

Heat oil in skillet and sauté onions and green pepper until lightly browned, then add more oil and sauté eggplant. Remove and do the same to the zucchini, tomatoes and mushrooms. Add a bit more oil if necessary. Combine all ingredients in a baking dish and bake at 400 °F (205 °C) for 30 minutes, uncovered. If it appears to be getting dry, cover with foil. May be served either hot or cold.
Yield: 6 servings

NOTE: Ratatouille freezes well in either one large container or smaller individual bags or containers.

Vegetable Soufflé

3	eggs (separated)	3
½ c.	White Sauce I or II (p. 81–82)	125 mL
1 c.	vegetables (cooked and chopped)	250 mL
	seasoning to taste	

Beat egg yolks until thick; add White Sauce and blend well. Add vegetables and season. Beat egg whites until stiff; gently fold in vegetable mixture. Pour into a greased 2-c. (500-mL) baking or soufflé dish. Bake at 325 °F (165 °C) for about 50 minutes.
Yield: 4 servings

Double-Baked Potatoes

4 medium	baking potatoes	4 medium
¼ c.	milk-free margarine	60 mL
½ c.	milk substitute	125 mL
	salt and pepper to taste	

Wash potatoes, and prick with a fork. Bake at 375 °F (190 °C) for 45 to 60 minutes, or until soft. Slice off about ½ in. (1 cm) across the top of each potato and discard tops. Scoop contents of each potato into a large mixing bowl. Add margarine, milk substitute, salt and pepper and beat with electric mixer at high speed for 2 minutes. Mix with any of the suggested mixers and refill the potato skins, or refill the skins with just the beaten potatoes. Top with any of the suggested toppers. Rebake potatoes at 425 °F (218 °C) until crusty, about 10 to 15 minutes.
Yield: 4 servings

Mixers	Toppers
Prepared mustard	Cornflake crumbs
Dill	Crumbled Italian sausage
Sweet pickle relish	Bacon bits
	Crushed garlic croutons

Potato Pancakes

6 to 8 medium	potatoes	6 to 8 medium
1 T.	onion, minced	15 mL
2	eggs	2
3 T.	flour	45 mL
1 t.	salt	5 mL
½ t.	baking powder	3 mL

Peel and grate potatoes. Add onion and let mixture stand about 15 minutes. Pour off liquid. Slightly beat eggs and blend into potato mixture. Add dry ingredients and mix well. Cook spoonfuls of mixture in a hot, well-oiled skillet. Serve with cold applesauce, Hot Apple-Pear Sauce (p. 83), or cinnamon and sugar.
Yield: 6 servings

Potato Soufflé

3 lbs.	potatoes	1.4 kg
½ c.	milk substitute	125 mL
¼ c.	water	60 mL
1 t.	salt	5 mL
¼ t.	white pepper	1.5 mL
2	egg yolks (beaten)	2
4 T.	milk-free margarine	60 mL
2	egg whites (stiffly beaten)	2

Cook potatoes in jackets until soft; drain and peel. Mash thoroughly. Heat milk substitute and water and set aside until tepid. Blend seasonings, egg yolks and 3 T. (45 mL) margarine until potatoes are well seasoned. Add enough milk substitute and water mixture to make potatoes creamy. Beat well using a hand mixer if desired. Fold in egg whites and pour mixture into a greased 2-qt. (2-L) casserole. Dot with remaining margarine. Bake at 375 °F (190 °C) for 30 minutes, or until brown.

Yield: 8 servings

Carrot Pudding

½ c.	milk-free margarine	125 mL
¾ c.	brown sugar	185 mL
3	eggs (separated)	3
1½ c.	flour	375 mL
1 T.	water	15 mL
1 T.	cinnamon	15 mL
½ t.	baking soda	3 mL
½ t.	baking powder	3 mL
1 t.	salt	5 mL
3 c.	carrots, grated	750 mL

Cream margarine and sugar. Add egg yolks, flour, water, cinnamon, baking soda, baking powder and salt. Blend thoroughly. Add carrots and blend. In a large bowl, beat egg whites until stiff. Gently fold carrot mixture into egg whites and fill a 9-in. (23-cm) square pan. Bake at 350 °F (175 °C) for 1 hour. Serve hot.

Yield: 4 servings

Green Bean Casserole

½ lb.	green beans, cut in 1-in. (2.5-cm) pieces	225 g
½ c.	mushrooms, sliced	125 mL
1 cube	TELMA mushroom soup	1 cube
¾ c.	cold water	185 mL
¼ c.	milk substitute	60 mL
¾ c.	cornflake crumbs or crushed Mild Garlic Croutons (p. 40)	185 mL

Toss beans and mushrooms in a 1-qt. (1-L) casserole. In a small saucepan, crush cube of mushroom soup in the water; add milk substitute. Bring to a boil and simmer for 5 minutes. Pour soup over beans and mushrooms, and top with cornflake or crouton crumbs. Bake at 350 °F (175 °C) for 1 hour. Add water if casserole becomes dry.
Yield: 4 servings

Creamed Vegetables

2 c.	vegetables (canned, cooked, fresh or frozen)	500 mL
1 c.	White Sauce I (p. 81)	250 mL

Heat vegetables in White Sauce or pour hot White Sauce over heated vegetables. White Sauce I makes 2 c. (500 mL); the leftover sauce can be frozen for later use.
Yield: 4 servings

Easiest Marinated Vegetables

Fill plastic bags with different vegetables, one type to a bag. Pour in enough of your favorite Italian dressing or vinaigrette to cover vegetables. Tie bags and refrigerate overnight. Before serving, poke a hole in the bottom of each bag and let marinade drain out. Discard bags. Arrange vegetables on a tray and serve cold. Try the following:

Green beans (raw or cooked)
Sliced zucchini (raw)
Hearts of palm (canned)
Artichoke hearts

Cherry tomatoes
Cooked carrots
Kidney beans (cooked)
Lima beans (cooked)

Soups

While clear soups do not include milk products, chowders, bisques and cream soups normally depend on them. With a good thick base and some imagination, cream soups can be made in almost any flavor, style and consistency. Kosher-pareve dehydrated soups can be made into cream soups using milk substitute or soy milk.

When buying soup, check the label. All these companies make milk-free soups: CAMPBELL'S, PEPPERIDGE FARM, LIPTON, KNORR SWISS, CROSSE & BLACK-WELL, GOODMAN'S, TELMA, TABACHNIK and GREAT AMERICAN.

Cream of Chicken Soup

2 c.	chicken stock or bouillon	500 mL
2	small potatoes (peeled and diced)	2
1	large carrot (peeled and sliced)	1
½ c.	celery, chopped	125 mL
¼ c.	celery leaves salt and white pepper to taste	60 mL

Bring stock or bouillon to a boil. Add vegetables, salt and pepper and return to a boil; cover and simmer for 25 minutes. Pour into a blender and liquefy. Serve hot. If soup is too thick, use milk substitute, water or bouillon to thin.
Yield: About 3 c. (750 mL)

Vichyssoise

½ c.	scallions, chopped	125 mL
	(reserve greens)	
1 T.	milk-free margarine	15 mL
4 cubes	chicken bouillon	4 cubes
3 c.	boiling water	750 mL
3 medium	potatoes	3 medium
	(peeled and diced)	
½ t.	salt	3 mL
¼ t.	white pepper	1.5 mL
⅓ c.	mayonnaise (optional)	85 mL

Brown scallions in margarine and set aside. Prepare bouillon by combining cubes and boiling water. Add potatoes and 2 c. (500 mL) of bouillon to scallions. Add salt and pepper and bring to a boil. Reduce heat, cover and simmer for 25 minutes. Cool and beat in a blender until thoroughly combined. The more you blend, the thicker the soup. Beat in mayonnaise if you wish an extra-thick soup. If you wish to thin the soup, add additional bouillon. Put in bowl or pitcher and chill overnight. Garnish with chopped scallion greens and serve cold.
Yield: About 1 qt. (1 L)

Cream of Vegetable Soup

1 c.	pureed vegetable	250 mL
	(raw or cooked)	
2 c.	White Sauce I	500 mL
	(p. 81)	
	water	
	salt and pepper	
	to taste	

Combine pureed vegetables with White Sauce, and add enough water to thin. Heat thoroughly and season.
Yield: About 3 c. (750 mL)

NOTE: Asparagus, carrots, celery, peas, potatoes and tomatoes can all be used in this recipe. If using tomatoes, use a 1-lb. (454-g) can.

Potato Soup Base for Chowder

3 medium	potatoes (peeled and diced)	3 medium
2 c.	chicken bouillon or stock	500 mL

Add diced potatoes to bouillon or stock and bring to a boil. Cover and simmer for 25 minutes. Blend on High in a blender or food processor to liquefy.
Yield: About 3 c. (750 mL)

Pacific Chowder

1 c.	Potato Soup Base	250 mL
	chicken bouillon or stock	
7-oz. can	tuna (drained and flaked)	198 g

Thin Potato Soup Base (recipe above) with bouillon or stock as desired, add flaked tuna, and heat.
Yield: About 2 c. (500 mL)

Clam Chowder

1 c.	Potato Soup Base	250 mL
	clam juice	
6.5-oz. can	clams (drained, rinsed)	184 g

Thin Potato Soup Base (recipe above) with desired amount of clam juice, add clams, and heat.
Yield: About 2 c. (500 mL)

Crab Bisque

1 c.	Potato Soup Base	250 mL
¼ c.	water	60 mL
1 c.	crab meat (flaked, cartilage removed)	500 mL
¼ c.	white wine	60 mL

Thin Potato Soup Base (recipe above) with water, add crab meat and wine, and heat.
Yield: About 2 c. (500 mL)

Tomato Bisque

1 small	onion (chopped)	1 small
¼ c.	green pepper, chopped	60 mL
1 T.	milk-free margarine	15 mL
3 medium	tomatoes	3 medium
	(peeled and diced)	
¼ c.	water	60 mL
1 cube	chicken bouillon	1 cube
½ t.	dried dill weed	3 mL
dash	salt	dash
1½ c.	tomato juice	375 mL

Sauté onions and pepper in margarine. Add tomatoes, water, bouillon cube, dill and salt. Cover and simmer for 20 minutes, then let cool. Beat in the blender until thoroughly combined; add juice and blend. Pour into a pitcher or bowl. Serve hot or cold.

Yield: About 4 c. (1 L)

NOTE: To peel tomatoes easily, drop whole tomatoes into boiling water for about 1 minute. Remove, cool and peel.

Sauces

Many prepared sauces are available at the supermarket; the safe list is too long to mention here. Look for these types of sauces: steak sauce, chili sauce, hot sauce, Bordelaise sauce and a variety of Chinese sauces like brown, soy, plum, and sweet and sour sauce.

Barbecue Sauce

1 c.	vinegar	250 mL
½ c.	ketchup	125 mL
¼ c.	Worcestershire sauce	60 mL
1 T.	oil	15 mL
20 drops	hot sauce	20 drops

Combine all ingredients in a saucepan and bring to a boil. Simmer for 15 minutes.
Yield: About 1½ c. (375 mL)

White Sauce I

2 T.	milk-free margarine	30 mL
2 T.	flour	30 mL
2 c.	chicken bouillon	500 mL
	salt and white pepper to taste	
1	egg yolk	1

Melt margarine in a saucepan, add flour, and blend well. Slowly pour in 1½ c. bouillon, stirring constantly, and add salt and pepper. When the mixture just boils, blend 2 T. (30 mL) of hot sauce with egg yolk and add this mixture to sauce. Stir constantly. Add more bouillon if necessary to thin to desired consistency.
Yield: About 2 c. (500 mL)

White Sauce II

2 T.	milk-free margarine	30 mL
2 T.	flour	30 mL
¼ t.	salt	1.5 mL
¾ c.	milk substitute	375 mL
¼ c.	water	60 mL

Melt margarine in a small pan. Remove from heat, add flour and salt, and stir until smooth. Combine milk substitute and water. Place pan over low heat. Add liquid gradually and stir until thick.
Yield: About 1 c. (250 mL)

Hollandaise Sauce

3	egg yolks	3
2 T.	lemon juice	30 mL
½ c.	milk-free margarine	125 mL

Beat egg yolks and lemon juice for 2 minutes with an electric mixer. Melt margarine in a saucepan and slowly pour hot margarine into egg mixture, beating at high speed until fluffy.
Yield: About 1 c. (250 mL)

NOTE: Hollandaise Sauce can be served with broccoli, asparagus, ham and eggs.

Brown Sauce (Gravy)

2 T.	milk-free margarine	30 mL
2 to 3 T.	flour	30 to 45 mL
2 c.	beef bouillon or stock	500 mL
½ t.	Chinese brown sauce **or** KITCHEN BOUQUET	3 mL

Melt margarine and blend in flour, stirring constantly until brown. Gradually add bouillon until mixture boils and thickens. Cook 3 to 5 minutes longer. Add brown sauce for color. Strain if necessary.
Yield: About 3 c. (750 mL)

Spaghetti Sauce

2 medium	onions, minced	2 medium
2 cloves	garlic, minced	2 cloves
¼ c.	olive oil	60 mL
1½ lb.	ground beef	675 g
two 6-oz. cans	tomato paste	two 170-g cans
2 c.	tomato juice	500 mL
2 t.	salt	10 mL
½ t.	white pepper	3 mL
2 t.	sugar	10 mL
½ c.	red wine (optional)	125 mL

Brown onions and garlic in oil; add beef and brown. Pour off fat. Add remaining ingredients and bring to a boil. Cover and simmer for 2 to 3 hours. Add wine if you wish.
Yield: About 3 c. (750 mL)

Hot Apple-Pear Sauce

8 to 10	McIntosh apples (peeled and cored)	8 to 10
2	pears (peeled and cored)	2
1 c.	water	250 mL
½ c.	sugar	125 mL
½ t.	cinnamon	3 mL

Slice apples and pears into a saucepan. Add water, sugar and cinnamon. Simmer until mixture is thoroughly cooked, about 1 hour, adding more water if necessary. Mash with a potato masher and serve.
Yield: 2 qt. (2 L)

NOTE: Apple-Pear Sauce may also be served cold. Cherry juice may be added for color, if desired.

CAKES, FROSTINGS, PIES AND COOKIES

Cakes

When a cake recipe calls for milk, you may substitute water, fruit juice, applesauce or other mashed fruit such as banana or pineapple, or a mixture of one-half water, one-half milk substitute.

If you're in a hurry, most DUNCAN HINES cake mixes are milk-free; devil's food, marble, yellow, lemon, angel food and sponge cake are some of the varieties to try. MANIS-CHEWITZ offers a milk-free chocolate chiffon cake mix; PILLSBURY PLUS mixes also are milk-free.

Chocolate Cake

⅔ c.	milk-free margarine	170 mL
1⅔ c.	sugar	420 mL
3	eggs	3
½ t.	vanilla	3 mL
2 c.	flour	500 mL
⅔ c.	cocoa powder	170 mL
1¼ t.	baking soda	6.5 mL
1 t.	salt	5 mL
¼ t.	baking powder	1.5 mL
1⅓ c.	water	335 mL

Place first 4 ingredients in mixing bowl and beat on High for 3 minutes. Combine dry ingredients and add alternately with water to creamed mixture. Pour into two greased and cocoa-powdered 9-in. (23-cm) round baking pans. Bake at 350 °F (175 °C) for 30 to 35 minutes. Let cakes cool in pans for 10 minutes, then invert onto wire racks to completely cool. Frost or glaze, or dust with confectioners' sugar.

Lemon Cake

1 c.	milk-free margarine	250 mL
1½ c.	sugar	375 mL
3	eggs	3
3 c.	flour	750 mL
½ t.	baking soda	3 mL
2 t.	baking powder	10 mL
½ t.	salt	3 mL
½ c.	milk substitute	125 mL
½ c.	water	125 mL
3 T.	lemon juice	45 mL
2 T.	lemon rind, grated	30 mL

Cream together margarine and sugar. Add eggs one at a time, beating well after each addition. In a small bowl, sift together flour, baking soda, baking powder and salt. In another small bowl, blend milk substitute, water and 1 T. (15 mL) lemon juice. Alternately add these mixtures to the creamed mixture. Add rind and remaining juice; blend well. Pour into a greased and floured 3-qt. (3-L) fluted tube pan. Bake at 325 °F (165 °C) for about 1 hour, or until toothpick inserted in center comes out clean. Cool cake for 15 minutes before removing from pan. Top with confectioners' sugar or your favorite icing if desired.

Yellow Cake

½ c.	milk-free margarine (softened)	125 mL
1½ c.	sifted flour	375 mL
¾ c.	sugar	185 mL
2½ t.	baking powder	13 mL
½ t.	salt	3 mL
1	egg	1
¾ c.	water	185 mL
1½ t.	vanilla	8 mL

In a large bowl, blend margarine, flour, sugar, baking powder and salt. Add egg and half the water and mix until just moist. Beat at medium speed until well blended. Add the rest of the water and vanilla. Beat again. Bake for 25 minutes at 375 °F (190 °C) in a greased and floured 9-in. (23-cm) square baking pan or fill 12 cupcake moulds and bake for about 15 minutes.

Pineapple Upside-Down Cake

3 T.	milk-free margarine	45 mL
¾ c.	brown sugar	185 mL
8½-oz. can	pineapple, sliced (reserving syrup)	241 g
⅓ c.	shortening	85 mL
½ c.	sugar	125 mL
1	egg	1
1½ t.	vanilla extract	8 mL
1 c.	flour	250 mL
1¼ t.	baking powder	6.5 mL
¼ t.	salt	1.5 mL

In a small pan, melt margarine. Add brown sugar and 1 T. (15 mL) pineapple syrup; set aside. Cream together shortening and white sugar; add egg and vanilla and beat until fluffy. Sift together flour, baking powder and salt, and add to creamed mixture alternately with remaining pineapple syrup. Using either an 8-in. (20-cm) square or 9-in. (22-cm) round baking pan, pour in brown sugar and margarine mixture. Arrange pineapple slices in the ungreased pan and cover them with batter. Bake at 350 °F (175 °C) for about 40 minutes. Cool 5 minutes and invert onto serving plate.

Chocolate Chip Applesauce Cake

1¾ c.	flour	435 mL
1 t.	baking soda	5 mL
¼ t.	salt	1.5 mL
1 t.	cinnamon	5 mL
½ c.	shortening	125 mL
1 c.	sugar	250 mL
2	eggs	2
1 c.	applesauce	250 mL
½ c.	raisins	125 mL
½ c.	chopped nuts	125 mL
1 c.	chocolate chips	250 mL

Sift together flour, baking soda, salt and cinnamon. In a separate bowl, cream shortening and sugar; add eggs one at a time, beating well after each addition. Alternately add flour mixture and applesauce to creamed mixture, beating well after each addition until smooth. Stir in raisins, nuts and half of chocolate chips. Pour batter into a greased 9- × 5-in. (23- × 13-cm) loaf pan. Sprinkle remainder of chocolate chips over batter. Bake at 325 °F (165 °C) for 1 to 1½ hours, or until done. Let cool in pan. Cover tightly with plastic wrap and store overnight before cutting.

Air Cakes

Many cake recipes do not contain milk and so do not require substitutions. These are so-called air cakes, like sponge and angel food. They are baked in ungreased pans so that the batter can cling to the sides as it rises. Since they are milk-free, these cakes can be safely ordered in restaurants. Here are two examples.

Jelly Roll

5	eggs (separated)	5
1 c.	sugar	250 mL
1 T.	lemon juice	15 mL
2 T.	lemon rind, grated	30 mL
1 c.	flour	250 mL
1 c.	jelly	250 mL
	confectioners' sugar	

In a large bowl, beat egg yolks well. Add sugar and beat. Add juice and rind. In a small bowl, beat egg whites until stiff. Add flour and egg white alternately to batter, beating well. Pour into a jelly roll pan lined with waxed paper until about ¼ in. (6 mm) deep. Bake at 375 °F (190 °C) for 12 to 15 minutes. Turn out on a damp towel. Trim off the crusty edges and spread with jelly. Roll up and cool. Sprinkle with confectioners' sugar and slice.

Sponge Cake

1½ c.	sifted flour	375 mL
1½ c.	sugar	375 mL
¼ t.	salt	1.5 mL
½ t.	baking powder	3 mL
6	eggs (separated)	6
1 t.	cream of tartar	5 mL
¼ c.	cold water	60 mL
1 t.	vanilla	5 mL
2 t.	lemon juice	10 mL
2 t.	lemon rind, grated	10 mL

In a small bowl, sift together flour, 1 c. (250 mL) sugar, salt and baking powder. In a large bowl, combine egg whites and cream of tartar. Beat until thick. Slowly add ½ c. (125 mL) sugar and beat until mixture is stiff. In a small bowl, combine egg yolks, water, vanilla, lemon juice and grated rind. Add this to dry mixture and beat about 1 minute. Fold slowly into egg whites, blending well. Pour into an ungreased 10-in. (25-cm) tube pan. Bake at 350 °F (175 °C) for 40 to 45 minutes. Invert pan and cool for 1 hour before removing cake from pan.

Frostings

Frostings are easily made with water or juice or a mixture of milk substitute and water. Don't underestimate the power of a glaze, either. Glazes make excellent frosting substitutes, as do marshmallow sauce, chocolate sauce and fruit sauce. Pour these over individual cake slices.

Lemon Frosting

½ c.	milk-free margarine (softened)	125 mL
3 c.	confectioners' sugar	750 mL
2 T.	water	30 mL
2 T.	lemon juice	30 mL
1 T.	lemon rind, grated	15 mL

Cream margarine and add remaining ingredients, beating until fluffy.
Yield: Enough to frost a 9-in. (23-cm) layer cake

Chocolate Glaze

3 T.	cocoa powder	45 mL
3½ T.	melted milk-free margarine	55 mL
1½ c.	confectioners' sugar	375 mL
1 t.	vanilla	5 mL
3 T.	boiling water	45 mL

Mix cocoa powder and margarine in saucepan and stir constantly over low heat until well blended. Stir in sugar and vanilla until crumbly. Add 1 t. (5 mL) of water at a time until glaze pours well; add more if necessary. Pour quickly over the top of the cake or spread evenly.
Yield: Enough glaze for a 9-in. (23-cm) layer cake

Chocolate Frosting I

3 c.	confectioners' sugar	750 mL
¾ c.	cocoa powder	185 mL
⅛ t.	salt	.5 mL
2 t.	vanilla	10 mL
⅓ c.	milk-free margarine, softened	85 mL
5 T.	milk substitute	75 mL

Combine sugar, cocoa, salt, vanilla and margarine, beating well. Slowly add milk substitute until frosting is of spreading consistency; add additional milk substitute if necessary.
Yield: About 2 c. (500 mL), enough to frost a 2-layer cake

Chocolate Frosting II

½ c.	milk-free margarine (softened)	125 mL
2 c.	confectioners' sugar	500 mL
1	egg yolk (well beaten)	1
⅓ c.	cocoa powder	85 mL

Cream margarine and sugar until fluffy. Add egg yolk and beat, then beat in cocoa powder. If frosting is too thick, add a little warm water.
Yield: Enough to frost a 9-in. (23-cm) layer cake

VARIATION: To make Mocha Frosting, add 2 T. (30 mL) instant coffee.

Banana Frosting

2 T.	milk-free margarine (softened)	30 mL
¼ c.	banana, mashed	60 mL
¼ t.	lemon juice	1.5 mL
1½ c.	confectioners' sugar	375 mL

Combine ingredients and beat until smooth.
Yield: Enough to frost a 9-in. (23-cm) layer cake

Some Special Cake Variations

Variation I

Instead of making a regular 9-in. (23-cm) layer cake, fill three 8-in. (20-cm) round pans for a triple-layer beauty. Frost generously between layers and on top, but not the sides.

Variation II

sponge cake
milk-free whipping cream
strawberries

Using a sponge cake, cut a circle in the top and scoop out the cake halfway down. Fill the cavity with a mixture of whipping cream and strawberries. Frost the top with this mixture as well.

Variation III

8-oz. container	milk-free whipping cream	227 g
½ t.	cocoa powder	3 mL
2 t.	instant coffee	10 mL
	angel food cake	

Combine whipping cream, cocoa powder and instant coffee, adding more to taste. Spread topping on an angel food cake and serve.

Variation IV

nonstick vegetable spray
berries of your choosing
layer cake
confectioners' sugar

Spray a fluted round 3-qt. (3-L) cake pan with a nonstick vegetable spray. Pour in fresh or frozen berries (with no juice). Pour layer cake batter on top of this and bake. Invert, and berries have topped a decorative Bundt cake. Sprinkle with confectioners' sugar. Lemon cakes make the most versatile batter for this one, blueberries the best berries.

Confectioners' Sugar Frosting
(White Glaze)

1 T.	milk-free margarine (softened)	15 mL
½ t.	vanilla	3 mL
dash	salt	dash
1 c.	confectioners' sugar	250 mL
2 T.	water	30 mL

Place margarine, vanilla and salt in a bowl. Add sugar and water alternately, beating after each addition until smooth. Add more water or sugar if needed for consistency.

Yield: Enough glaze for a 9-in. (23-cm) layer cake

Pies

Pie crusts and tart shells made with shortening or milk-free margarine are just as flaky as those made with butter. I have found that some of the milk-free margarines taste peculiar when used in pastry; MAZOLA salt-free margarine seems to produce the most pleasing taste.

Graham-cracker crusts, always milk-free, suffice nicely for many cream pies. For your favorite cream filling, try substituting milk-free ice cream, or use meringue for heavy cream. Since their fillings do not contain milk, lemon meringue and fruit pies are good choices when dining out—if you know that the crust has not been made with butter.

Prepared or homemade phyllo (Greek pastry dough) is milk-free, so it can be used in making strudels.

When buying prepared pie crusts, look for ORONOQUE ORCHARDS frozen pie crusts, JOHNSTON'S Graham Cracker or Chocolate Flavored Ready-Crust, and ATHENA or APOLLO phyllo dough.

Plain Pastry

1½ c.	sifted flour	375 mL
½ t.	salt	3 mL
½ c.	solid shortening or milk-free margarine	125 mL
5 T.	ice cold water	75 mL

Sift together flour and salt and cut in half the shortening until mixture is crumbly; cut in remaining shortening. Do not overmix. Add 1 T. (15 mL) water and gently toss. Repeat this until the mixture forms a ball. Flatten on a floured surface and roll to ⅛-in. (3-mm) thickness. Fit into a pie plate and prick. Bake at 450 °F (230 °C) for 10 to 12 minutes. Cool and fill.

Yield: One 9-in. (23-cm) pie crust or 4–6 tart shells

Graham Cracker Crust

1¼ c.	graham crackers, crushed	310 mL
3 T.	sugar	45 mL
6 T.	melted milk-free margarine	90 mL

Mix graham cracker crumbs with sugar. Stir into melted margarine and mix well. Press firmly onto bottom and sides of a 9-in. (23-cm) pie pan. Either chill 45 to 60 minutes or bake at 375 °F (190 °C) for about 6 minutes; cool before filling. **Yield:** One 9-in. (23-cm) pie crust

Strawberry Cream Pie

9-in.	Graham Cracker Crust (recipe above)	23-cm
8-oz. container	nondairy whipping cream	227 g
3-oz. pkg.	strawberry gelatin	85 g
1 c.	fresh strawberries, sliced	250 mL

Whip nondairy cream according to directions; set aside. Make gelatin according to speed-set directions; when thickened, mix with whipped cream, beating well. Fold in strawberries and pour mixture into pie shell. Chill until firm.

Lemon Meringue Pie

1¼ c.	sugar	310 mL
3 T.	cornstarch	45 mL
3 T.	flour	45 mL
1½ c.	hot water	375 mL
3	eggs (separated)	3
2 T.	milk-free margarine	30 mL
1 t.	lemon peel, grated	5 mL
⅓ c.	lemon juice	85 mL
9-in.	pie crust	23-cm
	Graham Cracker Crust (recipe above), or Plain Pastry (p. 93)	

Heat sugar, cornstarch and flour in a saucepan over medium

heat. Gradually add hot water, stirring constantly until mixture boils. Reduce heat and cook 5 to 6 minutes longer. Set aside. Slightly beat egg yolks and add a little of the hot mixture. Pour all of the egg mixture into saucepan and bring to a boil. Add margarine and lemon peel, then add lemon juice slowly, mixing well. Pour into a pie shell. Top with meringue (recipe below), and bake at 350 °F (175 °C) for 10 to 15 minutes, or until meringue is lightly browned.

Meringue

2	egg whites	2
½ t.	vanilla	3 mL
¼ t.	cream of tartar	1.5 mL
5 T.	sugar	75 mL

Mix egg whites, vanilla and cream of tartar. Beat until soft peaks form. Gradually add sugar and continue beating until meringue is stiff and shiny.

Chocolate Cream Pie

1 env.	unflavored gelatin	1 env.
¼ c.	cold water	60 mL
3	eggs (separated)	3
½ c.	sugar	125 mL
1 t.	vanilla	5 mL
1 T.	chocolate liqueur or rum	15 mL
6 T.	cocoa powder	90 mL
2 T.	milk-free margarine	30 mL
½ c.	water	125 mL
½ c.	sugar	125 mL
9-in.	Graham Cracker Crust (p. 94)	23-cm

Soften gelatin in ¼ c. (60 mL) cold water and set aside. Beat egg yolks until thick; beat in sugar and vanilla. In a small pan, over very low heat, melt margarine and add cocoa and ½ c. (125 mL) water. Stir until well blended. Add softened gelatin, stirring until dissolved. Beat chocolate mixture into egg yolks and add liqueur. Chill until almost set. Beat room-temperature egg whites until thick; gradually add ½ c. (125 mL) sugar, beating until stiff. Fold a little egg white into chocolate mixture. Then, slowly fold chocolate mixture into egg whites. Pour into a cool shell, and refrigerate until firm.

Chocolate Mousse

½ c.	milk-free margarine	125 mL
¾ c.	cocoa powder	185 mL
5 T.	cold water	75 mL
5	eggs (separated)	5
1½ c.	sugar	375 mL

Melt margarine in saucepan and add cocoa powder and water. Blend and let mixture cool slightly. Beat egg yolks in a bowl; add chocolate mixture. In a separate bowl, beat egg whites until stiff; add sugar and beat again. Fold one-quarter of the egg whites into the chocolate mixture. Add remaining egg whites a little at a time, blending very gently. Pour into a 9-in. (23-cm) glass bowl, and refrigerate. Mousse will be ready in 1 hour.

VARIATIONS:

1. Spoon mousse into 12 individual half-cup (125 mL) dessert dishes and refrigerate.
2. Line a springform pan with upright ladyfingers. Pour the mousse into the pan and refrigerate for several hours or overnight. Release the mousse and top with semisweet chocolate curls.
3. Place a dollop of mousse on a crepe. Fold in the sides and refrigerate. When you're ready to serve, top with milk-free whipped cream.

Mom's Apple Pie

6 to 8 large	Northern Spy apples (peeled and cored)	6 to 8 large
1 c.	sugar	250 mL
2 t.	cinnamon	10 mL
2 T.	flour	30 mL
two 9-in.	Plain Pastry pie crusts (p. 93)	two 23-cm
3 T.	milk-free margarine	45 mL

Thinly slice apples and mix with sugar, cinnamon and flour. Fill an unbaked pastry shell and dot filling with margarine. Cover with top crust; seal and make slits in the top. Bake at 400 °F (205 °C) for about 1 hour.

Cookies

A wide variety of cookie recipes don't require milk and taste just as good when milk-free margarine or solid shortening is substituted for butter: chocolate chip cookies, peanut butter cookies, ginger cookies, refrigerator cookies, spice cookies and brownies are just a few examples. If your favorite cookie recipe uses milk, substitute a mixture of one-half water, one-half milk substitute.

Many commercially available cookies and cookie mixes are also milk-free. SUNSHINE Animal Crackers, KEEBLER Pecan Sandies, Girl Scout shortbread cookies, many STELLA D'ORO cookies, NABISCO Ginger Snaps, NESTLÉ chocolate chip and peanut butter cookie mixes, QUAKER OATS oatmeal cookie mix and PILLSBURY PLUS cookie mixes are some of the milk-free products found in the supermarket.

Sugar Cookies

2 c.	sifted flour	500 mL
1½ t.	baking powder	8 mL
½ t.	salt	3 mL
½ c.	milk-free margarine	125 mL
¾ c.	sugar	185 mL
1	egg	1
1 t.	vanilla	5 mL
1 T.	warm water	15 mL
	sugar	

Sift together first 3 ingredients and set aside. In a large bowl, cream margarine and sugar; add egg, vanilla and water. Beat well. Add dry ingredients and blend well. Refrigerate for about 1 hour. Roll to ¼-in. (6-mm) thickness and shape with cookie cutters. Sprinkle with sugar. Bake on an ungreased cookie sheet at 375 °F (190 °C) for about 8 minutes.
Yield: About 48 cookies

Cinnamon Cookies

2¾ c.	sifted flour	685 mL
2 t.	cream of tartar	10 mL
1 t.	baking soda	5 mL
½ t.	salt	3 mL
1 c.	milk-free margarine	250 mL
1⅓ c.	sugar	335 mL
2	eggs	2
¼ c.	cinnamon	60 mL
½ c.	sugar	125 mL

Sift together first 4 ingredients and set aside. Cream margarine and sugar; add eggs. Gradually add dry ingredients. Chill dough for 1 hour. Roll into 1-in. (2.5-cm) balls; then roll in a mixture of cinnamon and sugar. Place about 2 in. (5 cm) apart on an ungreased cookie sheet. Bake at 400 °F (205 °C) for about 8 minutes, or until lightly browned.
Yield: About 60 cookies

Peanut Butter and Jelly Cookies

½ c.	milk-free margarine	125 mL
½ c.	creamy peanut butter	125 mL
½ c.	sugar	125 mL
½ c.	brown sugar	125 mL
1	egg	1
½ t.	vanilla	3 mL
1 c.	flour	250 mL
¾ t.	baking soda	4 mL
¼ t.	salt	1.5 mL
	your favorite jelly	

Cream margarine, peanut butter and sugars until smooth. Add egg and vanilla. Sift together dry ingredients and blend into creamed mixture. Shape into 1-in. (2.5-cm) balls and place on an ungreased cookie sheet. Press each cookie with a fork. Put a small round of jelly in the middle of each cookie. Bake at 375 °F (190 °C) for 10 to 12 minutes. Cool slightly before removing from pan.
Yield: 36–48 cookies

Peanut Butter Chocolate Bars

12-oz. jar	crunchy peanut butter	360 g
2 c.	graham cracker crumbs	500 mL
¾ c.	melted milk-free margarine	185 mL
1 c.	confectioners' sugar	250 mL
12-oz. bag	semisweet chocolate chips	360 g

Mix together peanut butter, graham cracker crumbs, margarine and sugar. Press into an ungreased 13 × 9-in. (33 × 23-cm) pan. Bake at 375 °F (190 °C) for 5 to 7 minutes. Melt chocolate chips and pour on top of baked mixture. Let this cool. Refrigerate until completely chilled and cut into squares.
Yield: 24 bars

Best-Ever Brownies

½ c.	milk-free margarine	125 mL
1 c. plus 2 T.	sugar	250 mL , 30 mL
2	eggs	2
1 t.	vanilla	5 mL.
¾ c.	flour	185 mL
¼ t.	salt	1.5 mL
½ t.	baking powder	3 mL
½ c.	cocoa powder	125 mL
¾ c.	walnuts, chopped (optional)	185 mL
	confectioners' sugar (optional)	

Cream margarine and sugar; add eggs and vanilla and mix well. Sift together flour, salt and baking powder and add to creamed mixture. Blend in cocoa powder and add chopped nuts, if desired. Spread mixture into a greased 9-in. (23-cm) square pan and bake at 350 °F (175 °C) for 35 minutes. When cool, top with a sprinkling of confectioners' sugar.
Yield: 6 servings

ICE CREAM, SORBETS AND CANDIES

Ice Cream

Among the milk-free ices available in the supermarket are POPSICLES and kosher-pareve ices. Some ice cream chains make milk-free fruit ices, too.

None of the ice cream recipes in this chapter require an ice cream maker and can be made with an electric mixer, blender or food processor. For a milk-free topping, try HERSHEY'S or BOSCO chocolate syrup, or a variety of fruit sauces.

Light Strawberry Ice Cream

16-oz. container	milk substitute	454 g
½ c.	sugar	125 mL
2 t.	vanilla	10 mL
1	egg (separated)	1
16-oz. pkg.	frozen strawberries with syrup	454 mL

In a blender, whip the milk substitute for 2 minutes. Turn off blender and add sugar, vanilla, egg yolk and strawberries. Whip for 30 seconds, put into a bowl, and freeze for 30 minutes. In a small bowl, beat egg white until stiff. Fold into ice cream and refreeze in a plastic-covered container.

Yield: 2 qt. (2 L)

VARIATIONS: Blueberries, raspberries or boysenberries may be substituted for strawberries. This ice cream makes a tasty pie filling. After initial 30 minutes in freezer, spoon ice cream into a chilled prepared pie shell and freeze until firm.

Vanilla Milk-Free Ice Cream

8-oz. container	nondairy whipping cream	227 g
½ c.	sugar	125 mL
1 t.	vanilla extract	5 mL
1	egg (separated)	1

Chill beaters and bowl in the freezer for 10 minutes before starting. Whip thawed topping for 2 minutes. Add sugar, vanilla and egg yolk, and freeze for 30 minutes. In a small bowl, beat egg white until stiff. Remove ice cream from freezer, fold in egg white and beat for 1 minute. Pour into plastic container, cover and freeze. Ice cream will be ready in 24 hours. **Yield:** 1 qt. (1 L)

VARIATIONS:

Chocolate Ice Cream

Add ¼ c. (60 mL) cocoa powder to ice cream before freezing for the first 30 minutes. Chopped nuts and semisweet chocolate bits can also be added.

Coffee Ice Cream

Add ¼ to ½ c. (60 to 125 mL) instant coffee to ice cream before freezing for the first 30 minutes.

Fruit-Flavored Ice Cream

Add 1 c. (250 mL) frozen fruit to ice cream before freezing for the first 30 minutes. Fresh fruit can also be added, but will probably require additional sugar.

French Vanilla Ice Cream

Follow recipe for Vanilla Milk-Free Ice Cream, increasing vanilla to 2 t. (10 mL) and using 2 egg yolks.

Sorbets

Sorbets are French sherbets made without milk. Sorbet recipes occasionally call for cream, but this can be easily omitted. They are very low in calories and can be served as appetizers, side dishes or desserts. Since they don't store well, make only what you will need. Before serving, thaw sorbets for 5 to 10 minutes.

In making sorbets, make sure all of the ingredients and utensils, including the bowl, beaters and metal freezing container, are well chilled.

Basic Sorbet Recipe

3 c.	fruit or vegetable puree	750 mL
1 c.	syrup	250 mL
	or	
2 c.	fruit juice	500 mL
2 c.	syrup	500 mL

Add puree or juice to chilled syrup (recipe below). Pour into a 9-in. (23-cm) metal cake pan and freeze for 30 minutes. Remove and thaw for 10 minutes, then pour into a chilled bowl; beat mixture for 2 minutes. Scoop into cups of a metal muffin tin and freeze.
Yield: 1 qt. (1 L)

Sorbet Syrup

⅔ c.	water	170 mL
⅔ c.	sugar	170 mL

Combine water and sugar in a small saucepan. Stir over medium heat until sugar is dissolved; do not let mixture boil. Pour syrup into a mixing bowl and chill thoroughly.
Yield: 1 c. (250 mL)

Follow the Basic Sorbet Recipe and use your imagination to make many other flavors using fruit juice or fresh or thawed fruit.

Candies

Since milk chocolate is not included in a lactose-free diet, semisweet chocolate can be used instead. Both HERSHEY and NESTLÉ make semisweet chocolate chips. Do not buy artificial chocolate chips.

When buying candy, look for hard candies, milk-free carob bars (found in health-food stores), sugared nuts, JORDAN almonds, red candied apples, CRACKER JACKS, SWITZER'S red licorice, CHUCKLES, BRACH'S Spearmint Leaves and Orange Slices, DESTON'S and SCHRAFFT'S thin mints and NABISCO Junior Mints.

Peanut Brittle

1 c.	sugar	250 mL
½ c.	shelled peanuts, chopped	125 mL
2 pinches	salt	2 pinches

Melt sugar over low heat until golden brown. Remove from heat and add nuts and salt; blend. Pour onto a greased pan in a thin sheet. Let cool thoroughly, then break into pieces.

Glazed Nuts

1 c.	shelled nuts, whole (walnuts, almonds or pecans, or a combination of these)	250 mL
½ c.	sugar	125 mL
2 T.	milk-free margarine	30 mL
½ t.	vanilla extract	3 mL

Combine nuts, sugar and margarine in a heavy skillet. Cook over medium heat, stirring constantly for about 15 minutes. Nuts should be well coated and the sugar browned. Stir in vanilla. Spread nuts on ungreased foil and cool. When cooled, break into clusters.
Yield: 1½ c. (375 mL)

Party Blend

1 c.	crunchy cereal	250 mL
1 c.	shelled sunflower seeds (salted)	250 mL
1 c.	dark raisins	250 mL
1 c.	dates, chopped	250 mL
1 c.	broken pretzel sticks	250 mL
1 c.	salted peanuts	250 mL

Combine ingredients in a bowl, mix well and serve.
Yield: 6 c. (1.5 L)

Frozen Banana

1 large	banana	1 large
2	ice cream sticks	2
½ c.	semisweet chocolate bits (melted)	125 mL
	nuts, chopped	

Cut the banana in half crosswise. Insert ice cream sticks in cut ends. Cover with plastic wrap and freeze. When frozen, remove wrap, dip in melted chocolate bits and roll in nuts.
Yield: 2 servings

Chocolate Almond Marshmallows

6-oz. pkg.	semisweet chocolate bits	170 g
2 T.	milk-free margarine	30 mL
1	egg (slightly beaten)	1
1 c.	confectioners' sugar	250 mL
2 c.	miniature marshmallows	500 mL
1 c.	ground almonds	250 mL

Melt chocolate bits and margarine over low heat. Remove and blend in egg. Add sugar and marshmallows, blending well. Shape into 1-in. (2.5-cm) balls, roll in nuts, and chill.
Yield: 30 clusters

Substitutions

1 c. (250 mL) milk	½ c. (125 mL) milk substitute plus ½ c. (125 mL) water ½ c. (125 mL) juice plus ½ c. (125 mL) water for baking: 1 c. (125 mL) water plus 2 T. (30 mL) milk-free margarine in yeast dough: 1 c. (250 mL) ginger ale
1 c. (250 mL) buttermilk or sour milk	½ c. (125 mL) milk substitute plus ½ c. (125 mL) water plus 1 T. (15 mL) lemon juice or vinegar
light cream	milk substitute
heavy cream	milk-free whipping cream or meringue
sour cream	plain yogurt mayonnaise
cream cheese	mayonnaise
1 oz. (28 g) baking chocolate	3 T. (45 mL) cocoa powder plus 1 T. (15 mL) milk-free margarine

FOOD AND NUTRITION BOARD, NATIONAL ACADEMY OF SCIENCES
NATIONAL RESEARCH COUNCIL RECOMMENDED DAILY DIETARY ALLOWANCES,[a] Revised 1980
Designed for the maintenance of good nutrition of practically all healthy people in the U.S.A.

	Age (years)	Weight (kg)	Weight (lb)	Height (cm)	Height (in)	Protein (g)	Fat-Soluble Vitamins Vita-min A (μg^{a-1} RE)[b]	Vita-min D (μg)[c]	Vita-min E (mg α-TE)[d]	Water-Soluble Vitamins Vita-min C (mg)	Thia-min (mg)	Ribo-flavin (mg)	Niacin (mg NE)[e]	Vita-min B-6 (mg)	Fola-cin[f] (μg)	Vitamin B-12 (μg)
Infants	0.0–0.5	6	13	60	24	kg × 2.2	420	10	3	35	0.3	0.4	6	0.3	30	0.5[g]
	0.5–1.0	9	20	71	28	kg × 2.0	400	10	4	35	0.5	0.6	8	0.6	45	1.5
Children	1–3	13	29	90	35	23	400	10	5	45	0.7	0.8	9	0.9	100	2.0
	4–6	20	44	112	44	30	500	10	6	45	0.9	1.0	11	1.3	200	2.5
	7–10	28	62	132	52	34	700	10	7	45	1.2	1.4	16	1.6	300	3.0
Males	11–14	45	99	157	62	45	1000	10	8	50	1.4	1.6	18	1.8	400	3.0
	15–18	66	145	176	69	56	1000	10	10	60	1.4	1.7	18	2.0	400	3.0
	19–22	70	154	177	70	56	1000	7.5	10	60	1.5	1.7	19	2.2	400	3.0
	23–50	70	154	178	70	56	1000	5	10	60	1.4	1.6	18	2.2	400	3.0
	51+	70	154	178	70	56	1000	5	10	60	1.2	1.4	16	2.2	400	3.0
Females	11–14	46	101	157	62	46	800	10	8	50	1.1	1.3	15	1.8	400	3.0
	15–18	55	120	163	64	46	800	10	8	60	1.1	1.3	14	2.0	400	3.0
	19–22	55	120	163	64	44	800	7.5	8	60	1.1	1.3	14	2.0	400	3.0
	23–50	55	120	163	64	44	800	5	8	60	1.0	1.2	13	2.0	400	3.0
	51+	55	120	163	64	44	800	5	8	60	1.0	1.2	13	2.0	400	3.0
Pregnant						+30	+200	+5	+2	+20	+0.4	+0.3	+2	+0.6	+400	+1.0
Lactating						+20	+400	+5	+3	+40	+0.5	+0.5	+5	+0.5	+100	+1.0

[a] The allowances are intended to provide individual variations among most normal persons as they live in the United States under usual environmental stresses. Diets should be based on a variety of common foods in order to provide other nutrients for which human requirements have been less well defined.

[a-1] μg = microgram

[b] Retinol equivalents. 1 retinol equivalent = 1 μg retinol or 6 μg β carotene (a provitamin A carotenoid).

[c] As cholecalciferol (a form of vitamin D). 10 μg cholecalciferol = 400 IU (international units) of vitamin D.

[d] α-tocopherol equivalents. 1 mg d-α tocopherol = 1α-TE.

[e] 1 NE (niacin equivalent) is equal to 1 mg of niacin or 60 mg of dietary tryptophan.

[f] The folacin allowances refer to dietary sources as determined by *Lactobacillus casei* assay after treatment with enzymes (conjugases) to make polyglutamyl forms of the vitamin available to the test organism.

[g] The recommended dietary allowance for vitamin B-12 in infants is based on average concentration of the vitamin in human milk. The allowances after weaning are based on energy intake (as recommended by the American Academy of Pediatrics) and consideration of other factors, such as intestinal absorbtion.

FOOD AND NUTRITION BOARD, NATIONAL ACADEMY OF SCIENCES

NATIONAL RESEARCH COUNCIL RECOMMENDED DAILY DIETARY ALLOWANCES,[a] Revised 1980 (Continued)

Designed for the maintenance of good nutrition of practically all healthy people in the U.S.A.

	Age (years)	Weight (kg)	Weight (lb)	Height (cm)	Height (in)	Protein (g)	Minerals — Calcium (mg)	Phosphorus (mg)	Magnesium (mg)	Iron (mg)	Zinc (mg)	Iodine (µg)
Infants	0.0–0.5	6	13	60	24	kg × 2.2	360	240	50	10	3	40
	0.5–1.0	9	20	71	28	kg × 2.0	540	360	70	15	5	50
Children	1–3	13	29	90	35	23	800	800	150	15	10	70
	4–6	20	44	112	44	30	800	800	200	10	10	90
	7–10	28	62	132	52	34	800	800	250	10	10	120
Males	11–14	45	99	157	62	45	1200	1200	350	18	15	150
	15–18	66	145	176	69	56	1200	1200	400	18	15	150
	19–22	70	154	177	70	56	800	800	350	10	15	150
	23–50	70	154	178	70	56	800	800	350	10	15	150
	51+	70	154	178	70	56	800	800	350	10	15	150
Females	11–14	46	101	157	62	46	1200	1200	300	18	15	150
	15–18	55	120	163	64	46	1200	1200	300	18	15	150
	19–22	55	120	163	64	44	800	800	300	18	15	150
	23–50	55	120	163	64	44	800	800	300	18	15	150
	51+	55	120	163	64	44	800	800	300	10	15	150
Pregnant						+30	+400	+400	+150	h	+5	+25
Lactating						+20	+400	+400	+150	h	+10	+50

[a] The allowances are intended to provide individual variations among most normal persons as they live in the United States under usual environmental stresses. Diets should be based on a variety of common foods in order to provide other nutrients for which human requirements have been less well defined.

[h] The increased requirement during pregnancy cannot be met by the iron content of habitual American diets nor by existing iron stores of many women; therefore the use of 30–60 mg of supplemental iron is recommended. Iron needs during lactation are not substantially different from those of nonpregnant women, but continued supplementation of the mother for 2–3 months after parturition is advisable in order to replenish stores depleted by pregnancy.

Nutritive Values of Foods

TABLE 2.– NUTRITIVE VALUES OF THE EDIBLE PART OF FOODS

(Dashes (–) denote lack of reliable data for a constituent believed to be present in measurable amount)

Foods, approximate measures, units, and weight (edible part unless footnotes indicate otherwise)		Water	Food energy	Pro-tein	Fat
(A)		(B)	(C)	(D)	(E)
		Grams	Per-cent	Cal-ories	Grams	Grams

(Column headers row: Grams, Percent, Calories, Grams, Grams)

		Grams	Percent	Calories	Grams	Grams
DAIRY PRODUCTS (CHEESE, CREAM, IMITATION CREAM, MILK; RELATED PRODUCTS)						
Butter. See Fats, oils; related products.						
Cheese:						
Natural:						
Blue	1 oz	28	42	100	6	8
Camembert (3 wedges per 4-oz container).	1 wedge	38	52	115	8	9
Cheddar:						
Cut pieces	1 oz	28	37	115	7	9
Shredded	1 cup	113	37	455	28	37
Cottage (curd not pressed down):						
Creamed (cottage cheese, 4% fat):						
Large curd	1 cup	225	79	235	28	10
Small curd	1 cup	210	79	220	26	9
Low fat (2%)	1 cup	226	79	205	31	4
Low fat (1%)	1 cup	226	82	165	28	2
Uncreamed (cottage cheese dry curd, less than 1/2% fat).	1 cup	145	80	125	25	1
Cream	1 oz	28	54	100	2	10
Mozzarella, made with—						
Whole milk	1 oz	28	48	90	6	7
Part skim milk	1 oz	28	49	80	8	5
Parmesan, grated:						
Cup, not pressed down	1 cup	100	18	455	42	30
Tablespoon	1 tbsp	5	18	25	2	2
Ounce	1 oz	28	18	130	12	9
Provolone	1 oz	28	41	100	7	8
Ricotta, made with—						
Whole milk	1 cup	246	72	428	28	32
Part skim milk	1 cup	246	74	340	28	19
Romano	1 oz	28	31	110	9	8
Swiss	1 oz	28	37	105	8	8
Pasteurized process cheese:						
American	1 oz	28	39	105	6	9
Swiss	1 oz	28	42	95	7	7
Cream, sweet:						
Half-and-half (cream and milk)	1 cup	242	81	315	7	28
	1 tbsp	15	81	20	Trace	2
Light, coffee, or table	1 cup	240	74	470	6	46
	1 tbsp	15	74	30	Trace	3
Whipping, unwhipped (volume about double when whipped):						
Light	1 cup	239	64	700	5	74
	1 tbsp	15	64	45	Trace	5
Heavy	1 cup	238	58	820	5	88
	1 tbsp	15	58	80	Trace	6
Whipped topping, (pressurized)	1 cup	60	61	155	2	13
	1 tbsp	3	61	10	Trace	1
Cream, sour	1 cup	230	71	495	7	48
	1 tbsp	12	71	25	Trace	3

Chart courtesy of the United States Department of Agriculture, Home and Garden Bulletin #72.

108

	Fatty Acids											
Satu-rated (total) (F)	Unsaturated		Carbo-hydrate (I)	Calcium (J)	Phos-phorus (K)	Iron (L)	Potas-sium (M)	Vitamin A value (N)	Thiamin (O)	Ribo-flavin (P)	Niacin (Q)	Ascorbic acid (R)
	Oleic (G)	Lino-leic (H)										
Grams	Grams	Grams	Grams	Milli-grams	Milli-grams	Milli-grams	Milli-grams	Inter-national units	Milli-grams	Milli-grams	Milli-grams	Milli-grams
5.3	1.9	0.2	1	150	110	0.1	73	200	0.01	0.11	0.3	0
5.8	2.2	.2	Trace	147	132	.1	71	350	.01	.19	.2	0
6.1	2.1	.2	Trace	204	145	.2	28	300	.01	.11	Trace	0
24.2	8.5	.7	1	815	579	.8	111	1,200	.03	.42	.1	0
6.4	2.4	.2	6	135	297	.3	190	370	.05	.37	.3	Trace
6.0	2.2	.2	6	126	277	.3	177	340	.04	.34	.3	Trace
2.8	1.0	.1	8	155	340	.4	217	160	.05	.42	.3	Trace
1.5	.5	.1	6	138	302	.3	193	80	.05	.37	.3	Trace
.4	.1	Trace	3	46	151	.3	47	40	.04	.21	.2	0
6.2	2.4	.2	1	23	30	.3	34	400	Trace	.06	Trace	0
4.4	1.7	.2	1	163	117	.1	21	260	Trace	.08	Trace	0
3.1	1.2	.1	1	207	149	.1	27	180	.01	.10	Trace	0
19.1	7.7	.3	4	1,376	807	1.0	107	700	.05	.39	.3	0
1.0	.4	Trace	Trace	69	40	Trace	5	40	Trace	.02	Trace	0
5.4	2.2	.1	1	390	229	.3	30	200	.01	.11	.1	0
4.8	1.7	.1	1	214	141	.1	39	230	.01	.09	Trace	0
20.4	7.1	.7	7	509	389	.9	257	1,210	.03	.48	.3	0
12.1	4.7	.5	13	669	449	1.1	308	1,060	.05	.46	.2	0
—	—	—	1	302	215	—	—	160	—	.11	Trace	0
5.0	1.7	.2	1	272	171	Trace	31	240	.01	.10	Trace	0
5.6	2.1	.2	Trace	174	211	.1	46	340	.01	.10	Trace	0
4.5	1.7	.1	1	219	216	.2	61	230	Trace	.08	Trace	0
17.3	7.0	.6	10	254	230	.2	314	260	.08	.36	.2	2
1.1	.4	Trace	1	16	14	Trace	19	20	.01	.02	Trace	Trace
28.8	11.7	1.0	9	231	192	.1	292	1,730	.08	.36	.1	2
1.8	.7	.1	1	14	12	Trace	18	110	Trace	.02	Trace	Trace
46.2	18.3	1.5	7	166	146	.1	231	2.690	.06	.30	.1	1
2.9	1.1	.1	Trace	10	9	Trace	15	170	Trace	.02	Trace	Trace
54.8	22.2	2.0	7	154	149	.1	179	3,500	.05	.26	.1	1
3.5	1.4	.1	Trace	10	9	Trace	11	220	Trace	.02	Trace	Trace
8.3	3.4	.3	7	61	54	Trace	88	550	.02	.04	Trace	0
.4	.2	Trace	Trace	3	3	Trace	4	30	Trace	Trace	Trace	0
30.0	12.1	1.1	10	268	195	.1	331	1,820	.08	.34	.2	2
1.6	.6	.1	1	14	10	Trace	17	90	Trace	.02	Trace	Trace

TABLE 2.— NUTRITIVE VALUES OF THE EDIBLE PART OF FOODS - Continued

(Dashes (−) denote lack of reliable data for a constituent believed to be present in measurable amount)

(A)		(B)	(C)	(D)	(E)
		NUTRIENTS IN INDICATED QUANTITY			

(A)		(B)	(C)	(D)	(E)
Cream products, imitation (made with vegetable fat):					
Sweet:					
Creamers:					
Liquid (frozen)-----------	1 cup--------------	245	77	335	2	24
	1 tbsp-------------	15	77	20	Trace	1
Powdered------------------	1 cup--------------	94	2	515	5	33
	1 tsp--------------	2	2	10	Trace	1
Whipped topping:					
Frozen--------------------	1 cup--------------	75	50	240	1	19
	1 tbsp-------------	4	50	15	Trace	1
Powdered, made with whole milk.	1 cup--------------	80	67	150	3	10
	1 tbsp-------------	4	67	10	Trace	Trace
Pressurized--------------	1 cup--------------	70	60	185	1	16
	1 tbsp-------------	4	60	10	Trace	1
	1 tbsp-------------	12	75	20	Trace	2
Ice cream. See Milk desserts, frozen					
Ice milk. See Milk desserts, frozen					
Milk:					
Fluid:					
Whole (3.3% fat)-------------	1 cup--------------	244	88	150	8	8
Lowfat (2%):					
No milk solids added-------	1 cup--------------	244	89	120	8	5
Milk solids added:					
Label claim less than 10 g of protein per cup.	1 cup--------------	245	89	125	9	5
Label claim 10 or more grams of protein per cup (protein fortified).	1 cup--------------	246	88	135	10	5
Lowfat (1%):					
No milk solids added------	1 cup--------------	244	90	100	8	3
Milk solids added:					
Label claim less than 10 g of protein per cup.	1 cup--------------	245	90	105	9	2
Label claim 10 or more grams of protein per cup (protein fortified).	1 cup--------------	246	89	120	10	3
Nonfat (skim):					
No milk solids added------	1 cup--------------	245	91	85	8	Trace
Milk solids added:					
Label claim less than 10 g of protein per cup.	1 cup--------------	245	90	90	9	1
Label claim 10 or more grams of protein per cup (protein fortified).	1 cup--------------	246	89	100	10	1
Buttermilk-------------------	1 cup--------------	245	90	100	8	2
Canned:					
Evaporated, unsweetened:					
Whole milk-----------------	1 cup--------------	252	74	340	17	19
Skim milk------------------	1 cup--------------	255	79	200	19	1
Sweetened, condensed---------	1 cup--------------	306	27	980	24	27
Dried:					
Nonfat instant:					
Envelope, net wt., 3.2 oz[5]-	1 envelope----------	91	4	325	32	1
Cup[7]----------------------	1 cup--------------	68	4	245	24	Trace
Milk beverages:					
Chocolate milk (commercial):					
Regular---------------------	1 cup--------------	250	82	210	8	8

110

(I)	(G)	(H)	(I)	(J)	(K)	(L)	(M)	(N)	(O)	(P)	(Q)	(R)
22.8	.3	Trace	28	23	157	.1	467	[1]220	0	0	0	0
1.4	Trace	0	2	1	10	Trace	29	[1]10	0	0	0	0
30.6	.9	Trace	52	21	397	.1	763	[1]190	0	[1].16	0	0
.7	Trace	0	1	Trace	8	Trace	16	[1]Trace	0	[1]Trace	0	0
16.3	1.0	.2	17	5	6	.1	14	[1]650	0	0	0	0
.9	.1	Trace	1	Trace	Trace	Trace	1	[1]30	0	0	0	0
8.5	.6	.1	13	72	69	Trace	121	[1]290	.02	.09	Trace	1
.4	Trace	Trace	1	4	3	Trace	6	[1]10	Trace	Trace	Trace	Trace
13.2	1.4	.2	11	4	13	Trace	13	[1]330	0	0	0	0
.8	.1	Trace	1	Trace	1	Trace	1	[1]20	0	0	0	0
1.6	.2	.1	1	14	10	Trace	19	[1]Trace	.01	.02	Trace	Trace
5.[1]	2.1	.2	11	291	228	.1	370	[2]310	.09	.40	.2	2
2.9	1.2	.1	12	297	232	.1	377	500	.10	.40	.2	2
2.9	1.2	.1	12	313	245	.1	397	500	.10	.42	.2	2
3.0	1.2	.1	14	352	276	.1	447	500	.11	.48	.2	3
1.6	.7	.1	12	300	235	.1	381	500	.10	.41	.2	2
1.5	.6	.1	12	313	245	.1	397	500	.10	.42	.2	2
1.8	.7	.1	14	349	273	.1	444	500	.11	.47	.2	3
.3	.1	Trace	12	302	247	.1	406	500	.09	.37	.2	2
.4	.1	Trace	12	316	255	.1	418	500	.10	.43	.2	2
.4	.1	Trace	14	352	275	.1	446	500	.11	.48	.2	3
1.3	.5	Trace	12	285	219	.1	371	[3]80	.08	.38	.1	2
11.6	5.3	0.4	25	657	510	.5	764	[3]610	.12	.80	.5	5
.3	.1	Trace	29	738	497	.7	845	[4]1,000	.11	.79	.4	3
16.8	6.7	.7	166	868	775	.6	1,136	[3]1,000	.28	1.27	.6	8
.4	.1	Trace	47	1,120	896	.3	1,552	[6]2,160	.38	1.59	.8	5
.3	.1	Trace	35	837	670	.2	1,160	[6]1,610	.28	1.19	.6	4
5.3	2.2	.2	26	280	251	.6	417	[3]300	.09	.41	.3	2

TABLE 2.– NUTRITIVE VALUES OF THE EDIBLE PART OF FOODS · Continued

(Dashes (–) denote lack of reliable data for a constituent believed to be present in measurable amount)

Foods, approximate measures, units, and weight (edible part unless footnotes indicate otherwise)			Water	Food energy	Pro-tein	Fat
(A)			(B)	(C)	(D)	(E)
		Grams	*Per-cent*	*Cal-ories*	*Grams*	*Grams*
DAIRY PRODUCTS (CHEESE, CREAM, IMITATION CREAM, MILK; RELATED PRODUCTS)—Con.						
Lowfat (2%)-----------------	1 cup------------------	250	84	180	8	5
Lowfat (1%)-----------------	1 cup------------------	250	85	160	8	3
Eggnog (commercial)------------	1 cup------------------	254	74	340	10	19
Shakes, thick:[8]						
Chocolate, container, net wt., 10.6 oz.	1 container-----------	300	72	355	9	8
Vanilla, container, net wt., 11 oz.	1 container-----------	313	74	350	12	9
Milk desserts, frozen:						
Ice cream:						
Regular (about 11% fat):						
Hardened-------------------	1/2 gal---------------	1,064	61	2,155	38	115
	1 cup-----------------	133	61	270	5	14
	3-fl oz---------------	50	61	100	2	5
Soft serve (frozen custard)	1 cup-----------------	173	60	375	7	23
Rich (about 16% fat), hardened.	1/2 gal---------------	1,188	59	2,805	33	190
	1 cup-----------------	148	59	350	4	24
Ice milk:						
Hardened (about 4.3% fat)----	1/2 gal---------------	1,048	69	1,470	41	45
	1 cup-----------------	131	69	185	5	6
Soft serve (about 2.6% fat)	1 cup-----------------	175	70	225	8	5
Sherbet (about 2% fat)-------	1/2 gal---------------	1,542	66	2,160	17	31
	1 cup-----------------	193	66	270	2	4
Milk desserts, other:						
Custard, baked---------------	1 cup-----------------	265	77	305	14	15
Puddings:						
From home recipe:						
Starch base:						
Chocolate--------------	1 cup-----------------	260	66	385	8	12
Vanilla (blancmange)---	1 cup-----------------	255	76	285	9	10
Tapioca cream-----------	1 cup-----------------	165	72	220	8	8
From mix (chocolate) and milk:						
Regular (cooked)---------	1 cup-----------------	260	70	320	9	8
Instant-----------------	1 cup-----------------	260	69	325	8	7
Yogurt:						
With added milk solids:						
Made with lowfat milk:						
Fruit-flavored[9]----------	8 oz------------------	227	75	230	10	3
Plain--------------------	8 oz------------------	227	85	145	12	4
Made with nonfat milk------	8 oz------------------	227	85	125	13	Trace
Without added milk solids:						
Made with whole milk-------	8 oz------------------	227	88	140	8	7
EGGS						
Eggs, large (24 oz per dozen):						
Raw:						
Whole, without shell-------	1 egg------------------	50	75	80	6	6
White----------------------	1 white----------------	33	88	15	3	Trace
Yolk-----------------------	1 yolk-----------------	17	49	65	3	6
Cooked:						
Fried in butter------------	1 egg------------------	46	72	85	5	6
Hard-cooked, shell removed.	1 egg------------------	50	75	80	6	6
Poached-------------------	1 egg------------------	50	74	80	6	6
Scrambled (milk added) in butter. Also omelet.	1 egg------------------	64	76	95	6	7

112

	Fatty Acids		Carbo-hydrate	Calcium	Phos-phorus	Iron	Potas-sium	Vitamin A value	Thiamin	Ribo-flavin	Niacin	Ascorbic acid
Satu-rated (total) (F)	Unsaturated Oleic (G)	Lino-leic (H)	(I)	(J)	(K)	(L)	(M)	(N)	(O)	(P)	(Q)	(R)
Grams	Grams	Grams	Grams	Milli-grams	Milli-grams	Milli-grams	Milli-grams	Inter-national units	Milli-grams	Milli-grams	Milli-grams	Milli-grams
3.1	1.3	.1	26	284	254	.6	422	500	.10	.42	.3	2
1.5	.7	.1	26	287	257	.6	426	500	.10	.40	.2	2
11.3	5.0	.6	34	330	278	.5	420	890	.09	.48	.3	4
5.0	2.0	.2	63	396	378	.9	672	260	.14	.67	.4	0
5.9	2.4	.2	56	457	361	.3	572	360	.09	.61	.5	0
71.3	28.8	2.6	254	1,406	1,075	1.0	2,052	4,340	.42	2.63	1.1	6
8.9	3.6	.3	32	176	134	.1	257	540	.05	.33	.1	1
3.4	1.4	.1	12	66	51	Trace	96	200	.02	.12	.1	Trace
13.5	5.9	.6	38	236	199	.4	338	790	.08	.45	.2	1
118.3	47.8	4.3	256	1,213	927	.8	1,771	7,200	.36	2.27	.9	5
14.7	6.0	.5	32	151	115	.1	221	900	.04	.28	.1	1
28.1	11.3	1.0	232	1,409	1,035	1.5	2,117	1,710	.61	2.78	.9	6
3.5	1.4	.1	29	176	129	.1	265	210	.08	.35	.1	1
2.9	1.2	.1	38	274	202	.3	412	180	.12	.54	.2	1
19.0	7.7	.7	469	827	594	2.5	1,585	1,480	.26	.71	1.0	31
2.4	1.0	.1	59	103	74	.3	198	190	.03	.09	.1	4
6.8	5.4	.7	29	297	310	1.1	387	930	.11	.50	.3	1
7.6	3.3	.3	67	250	255	1.3	445	390	.05	.36	.3	1
6.2	2.5	.2	41	298	232	Trace	352	410	.08	.41	.3	2
4.1	2.5	.5	28	173	180	.7	223	480	.07	.30	.2	2
4.3	2.6	.2	59	265	247	.8	354	340	.05	.39	.3	2
3.6	2.2	.3	63	374	237	1.3	335	340	.08	.39	.3	2
1.8	.6	.1	42	343	269	.2	439	[10]120	.08	.40	.2	1
2.3	.8	.1	16	415	326	.2	531	[10]150	.10	.49	.3	2
.3	.1	Trace	17	452	355	.2	579	[10]20	.11	.53	.3	2
4.8	1.7	.1	11	274	215	.1	351	280	.07	.32	.2	1
1.7	2.0	.6	1	28	90	1.0	65	260	.04	.15	Trace	0
0	0	0	Trace	4	4	Trace	45	0	Trace	.09	Trace	0
1.7	2.1	.6	Trace	26	86	.9	15	310	.04	.07	Trace	0
2.4	2.2	.6	1	26	80	.9	58	290	.03	.13	Trace	0
1.7	2.0	.6	1	28	90	1.0	65	260	.04	.14	Trace	0
1.7	2.0	.6	1	28	90	1.0	65	260	.04	.13	Trace	0
2.8	2.3	.6	1	47	97	.9	85	310	.04	.16	Trace	0

TABLE 2.— NUTRITIVE VALUES OF THE EDIBLE PART OF FOODS - Continued

(Dashes (—) denote lack of reliable data for a constituent believed to be present in measurable amount)

(A)		(B)	(C)	(D)	(E)
		NUTRIENTS IN INDICATED QUANTITY			

FATS, OILS; RELATED PRODUCTS

		(B)	(C)	(D)	(E)
Butter:					
Regular (4 sticks per 1b):					
Stick (1/2 cup)-----------	1 stick-------------	113	16	815	1	92
Tablespoon ----------------	1 tbsp--------------	14	16	100	Trace	12
Pat (1 in square, 1/3 in high; 90 per 1b).	1 pat---------------	5	16	35	Trace	4
Whipped (6 sticks).					
Stick (1/2 cup)-----------	1 stick-------------	76	16	540	1	61
Tablespoon ----------------	1 tbsp--------------	9	16	65	Trace	8
Pat (1 1/4 in square, 1/3 in high; 120 per 1b).	1 pat---------------	4	16	25	Trace	3
Fats, cooking (vegetable shortenings).	1 cup---------------	200	0	1,770	0	200
	1 tbsp--------------	13	0	110	0	13
Lard--------------------------	1 cup---------------	205	0	1,850	0	205
	1 tbsp--------------	13	0	115	0	13
Margarine:					
Regular (1 brick or 4 sticks per 1b):					
Stick (1/2 cup)--------------	1 stick-------------	113	16	815	1	92
Tablespoon (about 1/8 stick)-	1 tbsp--------------	14	16	100	Trace	12
Pat (1 in square, 1/3 in high; 90 per 1b).	1 pat---------------	5	16	35	Trace	4
Soft, two 8-oz containers per 1b.	1 container---------	227	16	1,635	1	184
	1 tbsp--------------	14	16	100	Trace	12
Whipped (6 sticks per 1b):					
Stick (1/2 cup)--------------	1 stick-------------	76	16	545	Trace	61
Tablespoon (about 1/8 stick)-	1 tbsp--------------	9	16	70	Trace	8
Oils, salad or cooking:					
Corn------------------------	1 cup---------------	218	0	1,925	0	218
	1 tbsp--------------	14	0	120	0	14
Olive-----------------------	1 cup---------------	216	0	1,910	0	216
	1 tbsp--------------	14	0	120	0	14
Peanut----------------------	1 cup---------------	216	0	1,910	0	216
	1 tbsp--------------	14	0	120	0	14
Soybean oil, hydrogenated (partially hardened).	1 cup---------------	218	0	1,925	0	218
	1 tbsp--------------	14	0	120	0	14
Soybean-cottonseed oil blend, hydrogenated.	1 cup---------------	218	0	1,925	0	218
	1 tbsp--------------	14	0	120	0	14
Salad dressings:					
Commercial:					
Blue cheese:					
Regular--------------------	1 tbsp--------------	15	32	75	1	8
Low calorie (5 Cal per tsp)	1 tbsp--------------	16	84	10	Trace	1
French:					
Regular--------------------	1 tbsp--------------	16	39	65	Trace	6
Low calorie (5 Cal per tsp)	1 tbsp--------------	16	77	15	Trace	1
Italian:					
Regular--------------------	1 tbsp--------------	15	28	85	Trace	9
Low calorie (2 Cal per tsp)	1 tbsp--------------	15	90	10	Trace	1
Mayonnaise------------------	1 tbsp--------------	14	15	100	Trace	11
Mayonnaise type:					
Regular--------------------	1 tbsp--------------	15	41	65	Trace	6
Low calorie (8 Cal per tsp)	1 tbsp--------------	16	81	20	Trace	2
Tartar sauce, regular-------	1 tbsp--------------	14	34	75	Trace	8
Thousand Island:					
Regular--------------------	1 tbsp--------------	16	32	80	Trace	8
Low calorie (10 Cal per tsp)	1 tbsp--------------	15	68	25	Trace	2

(F)	(G)	(H)	(I)	(J)	(K)	(L)	(M)	(N)	(O)	(P)	(Q)	(R)
57.3	23.1	2.1	Trace	27	26	.2	29	[11]3,470	.01	.04	Trace	0
7.2	2.9	.3	Trace	3	3	Trace	4	[11]430	Trace	Trace	Trace	0
2.5	1.0	.1	Trace	1	1	Trace	1	[11]150	Trace	Trace	Trace	0
38.2	15.4	1.4	Trace	18	17	.1	20	[11]2,310	Trace	.03	Trace	0
4.7	1.9	.2	Trace	2	2	Trace	2	[11]290	Trace	Trace	Trace	0
1.9	.8	.1	Trace	1	1	Trace	1	[11]120	0	Trace	Trace	0
48.8	88.2	48.4	0	0	0	0	0	—	0	0	0	0
3.2	5.7	3.1	0	0	0	0	0	—	0	0	0	0
81.0	83.8	20.5	0	0	0	0	0	0	0	0	0	0
5.1	5.3	1.3	0	0	0	0	0	0	0	0	0	0
16.7	42.9	24.9	Trace	27	26	.2	29	[12]3,750	.01	.04	Trace	0
2.1	5.3	3.1	Trace	3	3	Trace	4	[12]470	Trace	Trace	Trace	0
.7	1.9	1.1	Trace	1	1	Trace	1	[12]170	Trace	Trace	Trace	0
32.5	71.5	65.4	Trace	53	52	.4	59	[12]7,500	.01	.08	.1	0
2.0	4.5	4.1	Trace	3	3	Trace	4	[12]470	Trace	Trace	Trace	0
11.2	28.7	16.7	Trace	18	17	.1	20	[12]2,500	Trace	.03	Trace	0
1.4	3.6	2.1	Trace	2	2	Trace	2	[12]310	Trace	Trace	Trace	0
27.7	53.6	125.1	0	0	0	0	0	—	0	0	0	0
1.7	3.3	7.8	0	0	0	0	0	—	0	0	0	0
30.7	154.4	17.7	0	0	0	0	0	—	0	0	0	0
1.9	9.7	1.1	0	0	0	0	0	—	0	0	0	0
37.4	98.5	67.0	0	0	0	0	0	—	0	0	0	0
2.3	6.2	4.2	0	0	0	0	0	—	0	0	0	0
31.8	93.1	75.6	0	0	0	0	0	—	0	0	0	0
2.0	5.8	4.7	0	0	0	0	0	—	0	0	0	0
38.2	63.0	99.6	0	0	0	0	0	—	0	0	0	0
2.4	3.9	6.2	0	0	0	0	0	—	0	0	0	0
1.6	1.7	3.8	1	12	11	Trace	6	30	Trace	.02	Trace	Trace
.5	.3	Trace	1	10	8	Trace	5	30	Trace	.01	Trace	Trace
1.1	1.3	3.2	3	2	2	.1	13	—	—	—	—	—
.1	.1	.4	2	2	2	.1	13	—	—	—	—	—
1.6	1.9	4.7	1	2	1	Trace	2	Trace	Trace	Trace	Trace	—
.1	.1	.4	Trace	Trace	1	Trace	2	Trace	Trace	Trace	Trace	—
2.0	2.4	5.6	Trace	3	4	.1	5	40	Trace	.01	Trace	—
1.1	1.4	3.2	2	2	4	Trace	1	30	Trace	Trace	Trace	—
.4	.4	1.0	2	3	4	Trace	1	40	Trace	Trace	Trace	—
1.5	1.8	4.1	1	3	4	.1	11	30	Trace	Trace	Trace	Trace
1.4	1.7	4.0	2	2	3	.1	18	50	Trace	Trace	Trace	Trace
.4	.4	1.0	2	2	3	.1	17	50	Trace	Trace	Trace	Trace

TABLE 2.— NUTRITIVE VALUES OF THE EDIBLE PART OF FOODS - Continued

(Dashes (—) denote lack of reliable data for a constituent believed to be present in measurable amount)

Foods, approximate measures, units, and weight (edible part unless footnotes indicate otherwise)			Water	Food energy	Pro-tein	Fat
(A)			(B)	(C)	(D)	(E)
		Grams	Per-cent	Cal-ories	Grams	Grams
From home recipe:						
Cooked type[13]----------------	1 tbsp---------------	16	68	25	1	2
FISH, SHELLFISH, MEAT, POULTRY; RELATED PRODUCTS						
Fish and shellfish:						
Bluefish, baked with butter or margarine.	3 oz---------------	85	68	135	22	4
Clams:						
Raw, meat only----------------	3 oz---------------	85	82	65	11	1
Canned, solids and liquid-----	3 oz---------------	85	86	45	7	1
Crabmeat (white or king), canned, not pressed down.	1 cup---------------	135	77	135	24	3
Fish sticks, breaded, cooked, frozen (stick, 4 by 1 by 1/2 in).	1 oz---------------	28	66	50	5	3
Haddock, breaded, fried[14]-------	3 oz---------------	85	66	140	17	5
Oysters, raw, meat only (13-19 medium Selects).	1 cup---------------	240	85	160	20	4
Salmon, pink, canned, solids and liquid.	3 oz---------------	85	71	120	17	5
Sardines, Atlantic, canned in oil, drained solids.	3 oz---------------	85	62	175	20	9
Scallops, frozen, breaded, fried, reheated.	6 scallops----------	90	60	175	16	8
Shrimp:						
Canned meat--------------------	3 oz---------------	85	70	100	21	1
French fried[16]----------------	3 oz---------------	85	57	190	17	9
Tuna, canned in oil, drained solids.	3 oz---------------	85	61	170	24	7
Tuna salad[17]--------------------	1 cup---------------	205	70	350	30	22
Meat and meat products:						
Bacon, (20 slices per lb, raw), broiled or fried, crisp.	2 slices------------	15	8	85	4	8
Beef,[18] cooked:						
Cuts braised, simmered or pot roasted:						
Lean and fat (piece, 2 1/2 by 2 1/2 by 3/4 in).	3 oz---------------	85	53	245	23	16
Lean only ------------------	2.5 oz-------------	72	62	140	22	5
Ground beef, broiled:						
Lean with 10% fat-----------	3 oz ---------------	85	60	185	23	10
Lean with 21% fat-----------	2.9 oz -------------	82	54	235	20	17
Roast, oven cooked, no liquid added:						
Relatively fat, such as rib:						
Lean and fat (2 pieces, 4 1/8 by 2 1/4 by 1/4 in).	3 oz---------------	85	40	375	17	33
Lean only ----------------	1.8 oz-------------	51	57	125	14	7
Relatively lean, such as heel of round:						
Lean and fat (2 pieces, 4 1/8 by 2 1/4 by 1/4 in).	3 oz---------------	85	62	165	25	7
Lean only ---------------	2.8 oz-------------	78	65	125	24	3
Steak:						
Relatively fat—sirloin, broiled:						
Lean and fat (piece, 2 1/2 by 2 1/2 by 3/4 in).	3 oz---------------	85	44	330	20	27

	Fatty Acids											
Satu-rated (total)	Unsaturated		Carbo-hydrate	Calcium	Phos-phorus	Iron	Potas-sium	Vitamin A value	Thiamin	Ribo-flavin	Niacin	Ascorbic acid
	Oleic	Lino-leic										
(F)	(G)	(H)	(I)	(J)	(K)	(L)	(M)	(N)	(O)	(P)	(Q)	(R)
Grams	Grams	Grams	Grams	Milli-grams	Milli-grams	Milli-grams	Milli-grams	Inter-national units	Milli-grams	Milli-grams	Milli-grams	Milli-grams
.5	.6	.3	2	14	15	.1	19	80	.01	.03	Trace	Trace
—	—	—	0	25	244	.6	—	40	.09	.08	1.6	—
—	—	—	2	59	138	5.2	154	90	.08	.15	1.1	8
.2	Trace	Trace	2	47	116	3.5	119	—	.01	.09	.9	—
.6	0.4	0.1	1	61	246	1.1	149	—	.11	.11	2.6	—
—	—	—	2	3	47	.1	—	0	.01	.02	.5	—
1.4	2.2	1.2	5	34	210	1.0	296	—	.03	.06	2.7	2
1.3	.2	.1	8	226	343	13.2	290	740	.34	.43	6.0	—
.9	.8	.1	0	^{15}167	243	.7	307	60	.03	.16	6.8	—
3.0	2.5	.5	0	372	424	2.5	502	190	.02	.17	4.6	—
—	—	—	9	—	—	—	—	—	—	—	—	—
.1	.1	Trace	1	98	224	2.6	104	50	.01	.03	1.5	—
2.3	3.7	2.0	9	61	162	1.7	195	—	.03	.07	2.3	—
1.7	1.7	.7	0	7	199	1.6	—	70	.04	.10	10.1	—
4.3	6.3	6.7	7	41	291	2.7	—	590	.08	.23	10.3	2
2.5	3.7	.7	Trace	2	34	.5	35	0	.08	.05	.8	—
6.8	6.5	.4	0	10	114	2.9	184	30	.04	.18	3.6	—
2.1	1.8	.2	0	10	108	2.7	176	10	.04	.17	3.3	—
4.0	3.9	.3	0	10	196	3.0	261	20	.08	.20	5.1	—
7.0	6.7	.4	0	9	159	2.6	221	30	.07	.17	4.4	—
14.0	13.6	.8	0	8	158	2.2	189	70	.05	.13	3.1	—
3.0	2.5	.3	0	6	131	1.8	161	10	.04	.11	2.6	——
2.8	2.7	.2	0	11	208	3.2	279	10	.06	.19	4.5	—
1.2	1.0	.1	0	10	199	3.0	268	Trace	.06	.18	4.3	—
11.3	11.1	.6	0	9	162	2.5	220	50	.05	.15	4.0	—

TABLE 2.— NUTRITIVE VALUES OF THE EDIBLE PART OF FOODS - Continued

(Dashes (—) denote lack of reliable data for a constituent believed to be present in measurable amount)

(A)		(B)	(C)	(D)	(E)
NUTRIENTS IN INDICATED QUANTITY					
Lean only ----------------	2.0 oz----------------- 56	59	115	18	4
Relatively lean—round, braised:					
Lean and fat (piece, 4 1/8 by 2 1/4 by 1/2 in).	3 oz------------------- 85	55	220	24	13
Lean only ----------------	2.4 oz----------------- 68	61	130	21	4
Beef, canned:					
Corned beef-------------------	3 oz------------------- 85	59	185	22	10
Corned beef hash--------------	1 cup----------------- 220	67	400	19	25
Chili con carne with beans, canned.	1 cup----------------- 255	72	340	19	16
Chop suey with beef and pork (home recipe).	1 cup----------------- 250	75	300	26	17
Heart, beef, lean, braised------	3 oz------------------- 85	61	160	27	5
Lamb, cooked:					
Chop, rib (cut 3 per lb with bone), broiled:					
Lean and fat----------------	3.1 oz----------------- 89	43	360	18	32
Lean only ------------------	2 oz------------------- 57	60	120	16	6
Leg, roasted:					
Lean and fat (2 pieces, 4 1/8 by 2 1/4 by 1/4 in).	3 oz------------------- 85	54	235	22	16
Lean only ------------------	2.5 oz----------------- 71	62	130	20	5
Shoulder, roasted:					
Lean and fat (3 pieces, 2 1/2 by 2 1/2 by 1/4 in).	3 oz------------------- 85	50	285	18	23
Lean only ------------------	2.3 oz----------------- 64	61	130	17	6
Liver, beef, fried[20] (slice, 6 1/2 by 2 3/8 by 3/8 in).	3 oz------------------- 85	56	195	22	9
Pork, cured, cooked:					
Ham, light cure, lean and fat, roasted (2 pieces, 4 1/8 by 2 1/4 by 1/4 in).[22]	3 oz------------------- 85	54	245	18	19
Luncheon meat:					
Boiled ham, slice (8 per 8-oz pkg.).	1 oz------------------- 28	59	65	5	5
Canned, spiced or unspiced:					
Slice, approx. 3 by 2 by 1/2 in.	1 slice---------------- 60	55	175	9	15
Pork, fresh,[18] cooked:					
Chop, loin (cut 3 per lb with bone), broiled:					
Lean and fat---------------	2.7 oz----------------- 78	42	305	19	25
Lean only ------------------	2 oz------------------- 56	53	150	17	9
Roast, oven cooked, no liquid added:					
Lean and fat (piece, 2 1/2 by 2 1/2 by 3/4 in).	3 oz------------------- 85	46	310	21	24
Lean only ----------------	2.4 oz----------------- 68	55	175	20	10
Shoulder cut, simmered:					
Lean and fat (3 pieces, 2 1/2 by 2 1/2 by 1/4 in).	3 oz------------------- 85	46	320	20	26
Lean only ------------------	2.2 oz----------------- 63	60	135	18	6
Sausages (see also Luncheon meat):					
Bologna, slice (8 per 8-oz pkg.).	1 slice---------------- 28	56	85	3	8
Brown and serve (10-11 per 8-oz pkg.), browned.	1 link----------------- 17	40	70	3	6
Deviled ham, canned----------	1 tbsp----------------- 13	51	45	2	4
Frankfurter (8 per 1-lb pkg.), cooked (reheated).	1 frankfurter---------- 56	57	170	7	15
Meat, potted (beef, chicken, turkey), canned.	1 tbsp----------------- 13	61	30	2	2

(F)	(G)	(H)	(I)	(J)	(K)	(L)	(M)	(N)	(O)	(P)	(Q)	(R)
1.8	1.6	.2	0	7	146	2.2	202	10	.05	.14	3.6	——
5.5	5.2	.4	0	10	213	3.0	272	20	.07	.19	4.8	——
1.7	1.5	.2	0	9	182	2.5	238	10	.05	.16	4.1	——
4.9	4.5	.2	0	17	90	3.7	——	——	.01	.20	2.9	——
11.9	10.9	.5	24	29	147	4.4	440	——	.02	.20	4.6	——
7.5	6.8	.3	31	82	321	4.3	594	150	.08	.18	3.3	——
8.5	6.2	.7	13	60	248	4.8	425	600	.28	.38	5.0	33
1.5	1.1	.6	1	5	154	5.0	197	20	.21	1.04	6.5	1
14.8	12.1	1.2	0	8	139	1.0	200	——	.11	.19	4.1	——
2.5	2.1	.2	0	6	121	1.1	174	——	.09	.15	3.4	——
7.3	6.0	.6	0	9	177	1.4	241	——	.13	.23	4.7	——
2.1	1.8	.2	0	9	169	1.4	227	——	.12	.21	4.4	——
10.8	8.8	.9	0	9	146	1.0	206	——	.11	.20	4.0	——
3.6	2.3	.2	0	8	140	1.0	193	——	.10	.18	3.7	——
2.5	3.5	.9	5	9	405	7.5	323	[21]45,390	.22	3.56	14.0	23
6.8	7.9	1.7	0	8	146	2.2	199	0	.40	.15	3.1	——
1.7	2.0	.4	0	3	47	.8	——	0	.12	.04	.7	——
5.4	6.7	1.0	1	5	65	1.3	133	0	.19	.13	1.8	——
8.9	10.4	2.2	0	9	209	2.7	216	0	.75	.22	4.5	——
3.1	3.6	.8	0	7	181	2.2	192	0	.63	.18	3.8	——
8.7	10.2	2.2	0	9	218	2.7	233	0	.78	.22	4.8	——
3.5	4.1	.8	0	9	211	2.6	224	0	.73	.21	4.4	——
9.3	10.9	2.3	0	9	118	2.6	158	0	.46	.21	4.1	——
2.2	2.6	.6	0	8	111	2.3	146	0	.42	.19	3.7	——
3.0	3.4	.5	Trace	2	36	.5	65	——	.05	.06	.7	——
2.3	2.8	.7	Trace	——	——	——	——	——	——	——	——	——
1.5	1.8	.4	0	1	12	.3	——	0	.02	.01	.2	——
5.6	6.5	1.2	1	3	57	.8	——	——	.08	.11	1.4	——
——	——	——	0	——	——	——	——	——	Trace	.03	.2	——

TABLE 2.— NUTRITIVE VALUES OF THE EDIBLE PART OF FOODS - Continued

(Dashes (—) denote lack of reliable data for a constituent believed to be present in measurable amount)

Foods, approximate measures, units, and weight (edible part unless footnotes indicate otherwise)		NUTRIENTS IN INDICATED QUANTITY			
		Water	Food energy	Pro-tein	Fat
(A)		(B)	(C)	(D)	(E)
	Grams	Per-cent	Cal-ories	Grams	Grams
Pork link (16 per 1-lb pkg.), cooked.	1 link---------------- 13	35	60	2	6
Salami:					
Dry type, slice (12 per 4-oz pkg.).	1 slice--------------- 10	30	45	2	4
Cooked type, slice (8 per 8-oz pkg.).	1 slice--------------- 28	51	90	5	7
Vienna sausage (7 per 4-oz can).	1 sausage------------- 16	63	40	2	3
Veal, medium fat, cooked, bone removed:					
Cutlet (4 1/8 by 2 1/4 by 1/2 in), braised or broiled.	3 oz------------------ 85	60	185	23	9
Rib (2 pieces, 4 1/8 by 2 1/4 by 1/4 in), roasted.	3 oz------------------ 85	55	230	23	14
Poultry and poultry products:					
Chicken, cooked:					
Breast, fried,[23] bones removed, 1/2 breast (3.3 oz with bones).	2.8 oz--------------- 79	58	160	26	5
Drumstick, fried,[23] bones removed (2 oz with bones).	1.3 oz--------------- 38	55	90	12	4
Half broiler, broiled, bones removed (10.4 oz with bones).	6.2 oz--------------- 176	71	240	42	7
Chicken, canned, boneless-------	3 oz------------------ 85	65	170	18	10
Chicken a la king, cooked (home recipe).	1 cup---------------- 245	68	470	27	34
Chicken and noodles, cooked (home recipe).	1 cup---------------- 240	71	365	22	18
Chicken chow mein:					
Canned----------------------	1 cup---------------- 250	89	95	7	Trace
From home recipe-------------	1 cup---------------- 250	78	255	31	10
Chicken potpie (home recipe), baked, [19] piece (1/3 or 9-in diam. pie).	1 piece-------------- 232	57	545	23	31
Turkey, roasted, flesh without skin:					
Dark meat, piece, 2 1/2 by 1 5/8 by 1/4 in.	4 pieces------------- 85	61	175	26	7
Light meat, piece, 4 by 2 by 1/4 in.	2 pieces------------- 85	62	150	28	3
Light and dark meat:					
Chopped or diced------------	1 cup---------------- 140	61	265	44	9
Pieces (1 slice white meat, 4 by 2 by 1/4 in with 2 slices dark meat, 2 1/2 by 1 5/8 by 1/4 in).	3 pieces------------- 85	61	160	27	5

FRUITS AND FRUIT PRODUCTS

Apples, raw, unpeeled, without cores:					
2 3/4-in diam. (about 3 per lb with cores).	1 apple-------------- 138	84	80	Trace	1
3 1/4 in diam. (about 2 per lb with cores).	1 apple-------------- 212	84	125	Trace	1
Applejuice, bottled or canned[24]---	1 cup---------------- 248	88	120	Trace	Trace
Applesauce, canned:					
Sweetened----------------------	1 cup---------------- 255	76	230	1	Trace
Unsweetened--------------------	1 cup---------------- 244	89	100	Trace	Trace

Fatty Acids												
Satu-rated (total)	Unsaturated		Carbo-hydrate	Calcium	Phos-phorus	Iron	Potas-sium	Vitamin A value	Thiamin	Ribo-flavin	Niacin	Ascorbic acid
	Oleic	Lino-leic										
(F)	(G)	(H)	(I)	(J)	(K)	(L)	(M)	(N)	(O)	(P)	(Q)	(R)
Grams	Grams	Grams	Grams	Milli-grams	Milli-grams	Milli-grams	Milli-grams	Inter-national units	Milli-grams	Milli-grams	Milli-grams	Milli-grams
2.1	2.4	.5	Trace	1	21	.3	35	0	.10	.04	.5	——
1.6	1.6	.1	Trace	1	28	.4	——	——	.04	.03	.5	——
3.1	3.0	.2	Trace	3	57	.7	——	——	.07	.07	1.2	——
1.2	1.4	.2	Trace	1	24	.3	——	——	.01	.02	.4	——
4.0	3.4	.4	0	9	196	2.7	258	——	.06	.21	4.6	——
6.1	5.1	.6	0	10	211	2.9	259	——	.11	.26	6.6	——
1.4	1.8	1.1	1	9	218	1.3	——	70	.04	.17	11.6	——
1.1	1.3	.9	Trace	6	89	.9	——	50	.03	.15	2.7	——
2.2	2.5	1.3	0	16	355	3.0	483	160	.09	.34	15.5	——
3.2	3.8	2.0	0	18	210	1.3	117	200	.03	.11	3.7	3
12.7	14.3	3.3	12	127	358	2.5	404	1,130	.10	.42	5.4	12
5.9	7.1	3.5	26	26	247	2.2	149	430	.05	.17	4.3	Trace
——	——	——	18	45	85	1.3	418	150	.05	.10	1.0	13
2.4	3.4	3.1	10	58	293	2.5	473	280	.08	.23	4.3	10
11.3	10.9	5.6	42	70	232	3.0	343	3,090	.34	.31	5.5	5
2.1	1.5	1.5	0	——	——	2.0	338	——	.03	.20	3.6	——
.9	.6	.7	0	——	——	1.0	349	——	.04	.12	9.4	——
2.5	1.7	1.8	0	11	351	2.5	514	——	.07	.25	10.8	——
1.5	1.0	1.1	0	7	213	1.5	312	——	.04	.15	6.5	——
——	——	——	20	10	14	.4	152	120	.04	.03	.1	6
——	——	——	31	15	21	.6	233	190	.06	.04	.2	8
——	——	——	30	15	22	1.5	250	——	.02	.05	.2	[25]2
——	——	——	61	10	13	1.3	166	100	.05	.03	.1	[25]3
——	——	——	26	10	12	1.2	190	100	.05	.02	.1	[25]2

TABLE 2.— NUTRITIVE VALUES OF THE EDIBLE PART OF FOODS · Continued

(Dashes (—) denote lack of reliable data for a constituent believed to be present in measurable amount)

(A)		(B)	(C)	(D)	(E)
		NUTRIENTS IN INDICATED QUANTITY			
Apricots:					
Raw, without pits (about 12 per 1b with pits).	3 apricots-----------	107	85	55	1	Trace
Canned in heavy sirup (halves and sirup).	1 cup---------------	258	77	220	2	Trace
Dried:					
Uncooked (28 large or 37 medium halves per cup).	1 cup---------------	130	25	340	7	1
Cooked, unsweetened, fruit and liquid.	1 cup---------------	250	76	215	4	1
Apricot nectar, canned------------	1 cup---------------	251	85	145	1	Trace
Avocados, raw, whole, without skins and seeds:					
California, mid- and late-winter (with skin and seed, 3 1/8-in diam.; wt., 10 oz).	1 avocado------------	216	74	370	5	37
Florida, late summer and fall (with skin and seed, 3 5/8-in diam.; wt., 1 lb).	1 avocado------------	304	78	390	4	33
Banana without peel (about 2.6 per 1b with peel).	1 banana-------------	119	76	100	1	Trace
Blackberries, raw-----------------	1 cup---------------	144	85	85	2	1
Blueberries, raw------------------	1 cup---------------	145	83	90	1	1
Cantaloup. See Muskmelons					
Cherries:					
Sour (tart), red, pitted, canned, water pack.	1 cup---------------	244	88	105	2	Trace
Sweet, raw, without pits and stems.	10 cherries---------	68	80	45	1	Trace
Cranberry juice cocktail, bottled, sweetened.	1 cup---------------	253	83	165	Trace	Trace
Cranberry sauce, sweetened, canned, strained.	1 cup---------------	277	62	405	Trace	1
Dates:					
Whole, without pits-------------	10 dates-------------	80	23	220	2	Trace
Chopped-----------------------	1 cup---------------	178	23	490	4	1
Fruit cocktail, canned, in heavy sirup.	1 cup---------------	255	80	195	1	Trace
Grapefruit:					
Raw, medium, 3 3/4-in diam. (about 1 lb 1 oz):					
Pink or red with peel[28] ------	1/2 ----------------	241	89	50	1	Trace
White with peel[28]-------------	1/2 ----------------	241	89	45	1	Trace
Canned, sections with sirup-----	1 cup---------------	254	81	180	2	Trace
Grapefruit juice:					
Raw, pink, red, or white--------	1 cup---------------	246	90	95	1	Trace
Canned, white:					
Unsweetened-------------------	1 cup---------------	247	89	100	1	Trace
Sweetened--------------------	1 cup---------------	250	86	135	1	Trace
Frozen, concentrate, unsweetened:					
Undiluted, 6-fl oz can---------	1 can---------------	207	62	300	4	1
Diluted with 3 parts water by volume.	1 cup--------------	247	89	100	1	Trace
Grapes, European type (adherent skin), raw:					
Thompson Seedless---------------	10 grapes------------	50	81	35	Trace	Trace
Tokay and Emperor, seeded types-	10 grapes[30]----------	60	81	40	Trace	Trace
Grapejuice:					
Canned or bottled---------------	1 cup---------------	253	83	165	1	Trace
Frozen concentrate, sweetened:					
Undiluted, 6-fl oz can--------	1 can---------------	216	53	395	1	Trace
Diluted with 3 parts water by volume.	1 cup---------------	250	86	135	1	Trace
Grape drink, canned--------------	1 cup---------------	250	86	135	Trace	Trace
Lemon, raw, size 165, without peel and seeds (about 4 per 1b with peels and seeds).	1 lemon-------------	74	90	20	1	Trace

(F)	(G)	(H)	(I)	(J)	(K)	(L)	(M)	(N)	(O)	(P)	(Q)	(R)
—	—	—	14	18	25	.5	301	2,890	.03	.04	.6	11
—	—	—	57	28	39	.8	604	4,490	.05	.05	1.0	10
—	—	—	86	87	140	7.2	1,273	14,170	.01	.21	4.3	16
—	—	—	54	55	88	4.5	795	7,500	.01	.13	2.5	8
—	—	—	37	23	30	.5	379	2,380	.03	.03	.5	[26]36
5.5	22.0	3.7	13	22	91	1.3	1,303	630	.24	.43	3.5	30
6.7	15.7	5.3	27	30	128	1.8	1,836	880	.33	.61	4.9	43
—	—	—	26	10	31	.8	440	230	.06	.07	.8	12
—	—	—	19	46	27	1.3	245	290	.04	.06	.6	30
—	—	—	22	22	19	1.5	117	150	.04	.09	.7	20
—	—	—	26	37	32	.7	317	1,660	.07	.05	.5	12
—	—	—	12	15	13	.3	129	70	.03	.04	.3	7
—	—	—	42	13	8	.8	25	Trace	.03	.03	.1	[27]81
—	—	—	104	17	11	.6	83	60	.03	.03	.1	6
—	—	—	58	47	50	2.4	518	40	.07	.08	1.8	0
—	—	—	130	105	112	5.3	1,153	90	.16	.18	3.9	0
—	—	—	50	23	31	1.0	411	360	.05	.03	1.0	5
—	—	—	13	20	20	.5	166	540	.05	.02	.2	44
—	—	—	12	19	19	.5	159	10	.05	.02	.2	44
—	—	—	45	33	36	.8	343	30	.08	.05	.5	76
—	—	—	23	22	37	.5	399	([29])	.10	.05	.5	93
—	—	—	24	20	35	1.0	400	20	.07	.05	.5	84
—	—	—	32	20	35	1.0	405	30	.08	.05	.5	78
—	—	—	72	70	124	.8	1,250	60	.29	.12	1.4	286
—	—	—	24	25	42	.2	420	20	.10	.04	.5	96
—	—	—	9	6	10	.2	87	50	.03	.02	.2	2
—	—	—	10	7	11	.2	99	60	.03	.02	.2	2
—	—	—	42	28	30	.8	293	—	.10	.05	.5	[25]Trace
—	—	—	100	22	32	.9	255	40	.13	.22	1.5	[31]32
—	—	—	33	8	10	.3	85	10	.05	.08	.5	[31]10
—	—	—	35	8	10	.3	88	—[32]	[32].03	[32].03	.3	([32])
—	—	—	6	19	12	.4	102	10	.03	.01	.1	39

TABLE 2.— NUTRITIVE VALUES OF THE EDIBLE PART OF FOODS - Continued

(Dashes (—) denote lack of reliable data for a constituent believed to be present in measurable amount)

Foods, approximate measures, units, and weight (edible part unless footnotes indicate otherwise)		Water	Food energy	Pro-tein	Fat
(A)		(B)	(C)	(D)	(E)
	Grams	Per-cent	Cal-ories	Grams	Grams
Lemon juice:					
Raw------------------------------ 1 cup------------------	244	91	60	1	Trace
Canned, or bottled, unsweetened- 1 cup------------------	244	92	55	1	Trace
Frozen, single strength, un-sweetened, 6-fl oz can. 1 can------------------	183	92	40	1	Trace
Lemonade concentrate, frozen:					
Undiluted, 6-fl oz can---------- 1 can------------------	219	49	425	Trace	Trace
Diluted with 4 1/3 parts water by volume. 1 cup------------------	248	89	105	Trace	Trace
Limeade concentrate, frozen:					
Undiluted, 6-fl oz can---------- 1 can------------------	218	50	410	Trace	Trace
Diluted with 4 1/3 parts water by volume. 1 cup------------------	247	89	100	Trace	Trace
Lime juice:					
Raw------------------------------ 1 cup------------------	246	90	65	1	Trace
Canned, unsweetened------------- 1 cup------------------	246	90	65	1	Trace
Muskmelons, raw, with rind, without seed cavity:					
Cantaloup, orange-fleshed (with rind and seed cavity, 5-in diam., 2 1/3 lb). 1/2 melon -------------	477	91	80	2	Trace
Honeydew (with rind and seed cavity, 6 1/2-in diam., 5 1/4 lb). 1/10 melon -----------	226	91	50	1	Trace
Oranges, all commercial varieties, raw:					
Whole, 2 5/8-in diam., without peel and seeds (about 2 1/2 per lb with peel and seeds). 1 orange--------------	131	86	65	1	Trace
Sections without membranes------ 1 cup------------------	180	86	90	2	Trace
Orange juice:					
Raw, all varieties-------------- 1 cup------------------	248	88	110	2	Trace
Canned, unsweetened------------- 1 cup------------------	249	87	120	2	Trace
Frozen concentrate:					
Undiluted, 6-fl oz can-------- 1 can------------------	213	55	360	5	Trace
Diluted with 3 parts water by volume. 1 cup------------------	249	87	120	2	Trace
Orange and grapefruit juice:					
Frozen concentrate:					
Undiluted, 6-fl oz can-------- 1 can------------------	210	59	330	4	1
Diluted with 3 parts water by volume. 1 cup------------------	248	88	110	1	Trace
Papayas, raw, 1/2-in cubes-------- 1 cup------------------	140	89	55	1	Trace
Peaches:					
Raw:					
Whole, 2 1/2-in diam., peeled, pitted (about 4 per lb with peels and pits). 1 peach----------------	100	89	40	1	Trace
Sliced------------------------ 1 cup------------------	170	89	65	1	Trace
Canned, yellow-fleshed, solids and liquid (halves or slices):					
Sirup pack-------------------- 1 cup------------------	256	79	200	1	Trace
Water pack-------------------- 1 cup------------------	244	91	75	1	Trace
Dried:					
Uncooked---------------------- 1 cup------------------	160	25	420	5	1
Cooked, unsweetened, halves and juice. 1 cup------------------	250	77	205	3	1
Frozen, sliced, sweetened:					
10-oz container--------------- 1 container----------	284	77	250	1	Trace
Cup-------------------------- 1 cup------------------	250	77	220	1	Trace

124

	Fatty Acids											
Satu-rated (total)	Unsaturated		Carbo-hydrate	Calcium	Phos-phorus	Iron	Potas-sium	Vitamin A value	Thiamin	Ribo-flavin	Niacin	Ascorbic acid
	Oleic	Lino-leic										
(F)	(G)	(H)	(I)	(J)	(K)	(L)	(M)	(N)	(O)	(P)	(Q)	(R)
Grams	Grams	Grams	Grams	Milli-grams	Milli-grams	Milli-grams	Milli-grams	Inter-national units	Milli-grams	Milli-grams	Milli-grams	Milli-grams
—	—	—	20	17	24	.5	344	50	.07	.02	.2	112
—	—	—	19	17	24	.5	344	50	.07	.02	.2	102
—	—	—	13	13	16	.5	258	40	.05	.02	.2	81
—	—	—	112	9	13	.4	153	40	.05	.06	.7	66
—	—	—	28	2	3	.1	40	10	.01	.02	.2	17
—	—	—	108	11	13	.2	129	Trace	.02	.02	.2	26
—	—	—	27	3	3	Trace	32	Trace	Trace	Trace	Trace	6
—	—	—	22	22	27	.5	256	20	.05	.02	.2	79
—	—	—	22	22	27	.5	256	20	.05	.02	.2	52
—	—	—	20	38	44	1.1	682	9,240	.11	.08	1.6	90
—	—	—	11	21	24	.6	374	60	.06	.04	.9	34
—	—	—	16	54	26	.5	263	260	.13	.05	.5	66
—	—	—	22	74	36	.7	360	360	.18	.07	.7	90
—	—	—	26	27	42	.5	496	500	.22	.07	1.0	124
—	—	—	28	25	45	1.0	496	500	.17	.05	.7	100
—	—	—	87	75	126	.9	1,500	1,620	.68	.11	2.8	360
—	—	—	29	25	42	.2	503	540	.23	.03	.9	120
—	—	—	78	61	99	.8	1,308	800	.48	.06	2.3	302
—	—	—	26	20	32	.2	439	270	.15	.02	.7	102
—	—	—	14	28	22	.4	328	2,450	.06	.06	.4	78
—	—	—	10	9	19	.5	202	[34]1,330	.02	.05	1.0	7
—	—	—	16	15	32	.9	343	[34]2,260	.03	.09	1.7	12
—	—	—	51	10	31	.8	333	1,100	.03	.05	1.5	8
—	—	—	20	10	32	.7	334	1,100	.02	.07	1.5	7
—	—	—	109	77	187	9.6	1,520	6,240	.02	.30	8.5	29
—	—	—	54	38	93	4.8	743	3,050	.01	.15	3.8	5
—	—	—	64	11	37	1.4	352	1,850	.03	.11	2.0	[35]116
—	—	—	57	10	33	1.3	310	1,630	.03	.10	1.8	[35]103

TABLE 2.— NUTRITIVE VALUES OF THE EDIBLE PART OF FOODS · Continued

(Dashes (—) denote lack of reliable data for a constituent believed to be present in measurable amount)

(A)		(B)	(C)	(D)	(E)
			NUTRIENTS IN INDICATED QUANTITY		

Pears:
Raw, with skin, cored:

(A)		(B)	(C)	(D)	(E)
Bartlett, 2 1/2-in diam. (about 2 1/2 per lb with cores and stems).	1 pear----------------	164	83	100	1	1
Bosc, 2 1/2-in diam. (about 3 per lb with cores and stems).	1 pear----------------	141	83	85	1	1
D'Anjou, 3-in diam. (about 2 per lb with cores and stems).	1 pear----------------	200	83	120	1	1
Canned, solids and liquid, sirup pack, heavy (halves or slices).	1 cup----------------	255	80	195	1	1

Pineapple:

(A)		(B)	(C)	(D)	(E)
Raw, diced----------------------	1 cup----------------	155	85	80	1	Trace
Canned, heavy sirup pack, solids and liquid:						
Crushed, chunks, tidbits-------	1 cup----------------	255	80	190	1	Trace
Slices and liquid:						
Large, 2 1/4 tbsp liquid.----	1 slice--------------	105	80	80	Trace	Trace
Medium, 1 1/4 tbsp liquid.---	1 slice -------------	58	80	45	Trace	Trace
Pineapple juice, unsweetened, canned.	1 cup----------------	250	86	140	1	Trace

Plums:
Raw, without pits:

(A)		(B)	(C)	(D)	(E)
Japanese and hybrid (2 1/8-in diam., about 6 1/2 per lb with pits).	1 plum----------------	66	87	30	Trace	Trace
Prune-type (1 1/2-in diam., about 15 per lb with pits).	1 plum----------------	28	79	20	Trace	Trace
Canned, heavy sirup pack (Italian prunes), with pits and liquid:						
Cup--------------------------	1 cup[36]--------------	272	77	215	1	Trace
Portion-----------------------	3 plums; 2 3/4 tbsp liquid.[36]	140	77	110	1	Trace

Prunes, dried, "softenized," pits :

(A)		(B)	(C)	(D)	(E)
Uncooked-----------------------	4 extra large or 5 large prunes.[36]	49	28	110	1	Trace
Cooked, unsweetened, all sizes, fruit and liquid.	1 cup[36]--------------	250	66	255	2	1
Prune juice, canned or bottled-----	1 cup----------------	256	80	195	1	Trace

Raisins, seedless:

(A)		(B)	(C)	(D)	(E)
Cup, not pressed down------------	1 cup----------------	145	18	420	4	Trace

Raspberries, red:

(A)		(B)	(C)	(D)	(E)
Raw, capped, whole---------------	1 cup----------------	123	84	70	1	1
Frozen, sweetened, 10-oz container	1 container----------	284	74	280	2	1

Rhubarb, cooked, added sugar:

(A)		(B)	(C)	(D)	(E)
From raw------------------------	1 cup----------------	270	63	380	1	Trace
From frozen, sweetened-----------	1 cup----------------	270	63	385	1	1

Strawberries:

(A)		(B)	(C)	(D)	(E)
Raw, whole berries, capped-----	1 cup----------------	149	90	55	1	1
Frozen, sweetened:						
Sliced, 10-oz container------	1 container----------	284	71	310	1	1
Whole, 1-lb container	1 container----------	454	76	415	2	1
Tangerine, raw, 2 3/8-in diam., size 176, without peel (about 4 per lb with peels and seeds).	1 tangerine----------	86	87	40	1	Trace
Watermelon, raw, 4 by 8 in wedge with rind and seeds	1 wedge with rind and seeds[37]	926	93	110	2	1

GRAIN PRODUCTS

Bagel, 3-in diam.:

(A)		(B)	(C)	(D)	(E)
Egg--------------------------	1 bagel---------------	55	32	165	6	2
Water------------------------	1 bagel---------------	55	29	165	6	1

126

(F)	(G)	(H)	(I)	(J)	(K)	(L)	(M)	(N)	(O)	(P)	(Q)	(R)
—	—	—	25	13	18	.5	213	30	.03	.07	.2	7
—	—	—	22	11	16	.4	83	30	.03	.06	.1	6
—	—	—	31	16	22	.6	260	40	.04	.08	.2	8
—	—	—	50	13	18	.5	214	10	.03	.05	.3	3
—	—	—	21	26	12	.8	226	110	.14	.05	.3	26
—	—	—	49	28	13	.8	245	130	.20	.05	.5	18
—	—	—	20	12	5	.3	101	50	.08	.02	.2	7
—	—	—	11	6	3	.2	56	30	.05	.01	.1	4
—	—	—	34	38	23	.8	373	130	.13	.05	.5	2/80
—	—	—	8	8	12	.3	112	160	.02	.02	.3	4
—	—	—	6	3	5	.1	48	80	.01	.01	.1	1
—	—	—	56	23	26	2.3	367	3,130	.05	.05	1.0	5
—	—	—	29	12	13	1.2	189	1,610	.03	.03	.5	3
—	—	—	29	22	34	1.7	298	690	.04	.07	.7	1
—	—	—	67	51	79	3.8	695	1,590	.07	.15	1.5	2
—	—	—	49	36	51	1.8	602	—	.03	.03	1.0	5
—	—	—	112	90	146	5.1	1,106	30	.16	.12	.7	1
—	—	—	17	27	27	1.1	207	160	.04	.11	1.1	31
—	—	—	70	37	48	1.7	284	200	.06	.17	1.7	60
—	—	—	97	211	41	1.6	548	220	.05	.14	.8	16
—	—	—	98	211	32	1.9	475	190	.05	.11	.5	16
—	—	—	13	31	31	1.5	244	90	.04	.10	.9	88
—	—	—	79	40	48	2.0	318	90	.06	.17	1.4	151
—	—	—	107	59	73	2.7	472	140	.09	.27	2.3	249
—	—	—	10	34	15	.3	108	360	.05	.02	.1	27
—	—	—	27	30	43	2.1	426	2,510	.13	.13	.9	30
.5	.9	.8	28	9	43	1.2	41	30	.14	.10	1.2	0
.2	.4	.6	30	8	41	1.2	42	0	.15	.11	1.4	0

TABLE 2.— NUTRITIVE VALUES OF THE EDIBLE PART OF FOODS - Continued

(Dashes (—) denote lack of reliable data for a constituent believed to be present in measurable amount)

Foods, approximate measures, units, and weight (edible part unless footnotes indicate otherwise)		Water	Food energy	Pro-tein	Fat
(A)		(B)	(C)	(D)	(E)
	Grams	Per-cent	Cal-ories	Grams	Grams
Barley, pearled, light, uncooked- 1 cup------------------	200	11	700	16	2
Biscuits, baking powder, 2-in diam. (enriched flour, vegetable shortening):					
From home recipe--------------- 1 biscuit--------------	28	27	105	2	5
From mix---------------------- 1 biscuit--------------	28	29	90	2	3
Breadcrumbs (enriched):[38]					
Dry, grated-------------------- 1 cup------------------	100	7	390	13	5
Soft. See White bread					
Breads:					
Cracked-wheat bread (3/4 enriched wheat flour, 1/4 cracked wheat):[38]					
Loaf, 1 lb----------------- 1 loaf-----------------	454	35	1,195	39	10
Slice (18 per loaf)---------- 1 slice----------------	25	35	65	2	1
French or vienna bread, enriched:[38]					
Loaf, 1 lb----------------- 1 loaf-----------------	454	31	1,315	41	14
Slice:					
French (5 by 2 1/2 by 1 in) 1 slice----------------	35	31	100	3	1
Vienna (4 3/4 by 4 by 1/2 in) 1 slice----------------	25	31	75	2	1
Italian bread, enriched:					
Loaf, 1 lb----------------- 1 loaf-----------------	454	32	1,250	41	4
Slice, 4 1/2 by 3 1/4 by 3/4 in 1 slice----------------	30	32	85	3	Trace
Raisin bread, enriched:[38]					
Loaf, 1 lb----------------- 1 loaf-----------------	454	35	1,190	30	13
Slice (18 per loaf)---------- 1 slice----------------	25	35	65	2	1
Rye Bread:					
American, light (2/3 enriched wheat flour, 1/3 rye flour):					
Loaf, 1 lb----------------- 1 loaf-----------------	454	36	1,100	41	5
Slice (4 3/4 by 3 3/4 by 7/16 in). 1 slice----------------	25	36	60	2	Trace
Pumpernickel (2/3 rye flour, 1/3 enriched wheat flour):					
Loaf, 1 lb----------------- 1 loaf-----------------	454	34	1,115	41	5
Slice (5 by 4 by 3/8 in)---- 1 slice----------------	32	34	80	3	Trace
White bread, enriched:[38]					
Soft-crumb type:					
Loaf, 1 lb----------------- 1 loaf-----------------	454	36	1,225	39	15
Slice (18 per loaf)------- 1 slice----------------	25	36	70	2	1
Slice, toasted---------- 1 slice----------------	22	25	70	2	1
Loaf, 1 1/2 lb------------- 1 loaf----------------	680	36	1,835	59	22
Slice (24 per loaf)------- 1 slice----------------	28	36	75	2	1
Slice, toasted---------- 1 slice----------------	24	25	75	2	1
Cubes--------------------- 1 cup------------------	30	36	80	3	1
Crumbs-------------------- 1 cup------------------	45	36	120	4	1
Firm-crumb type:					
Loaf, 1 lb----------------- 1 loaf-----------------	454	35	1,245	41	17
Slice (20 per loaf)------- 1 slice----------------	23	35	65	2	1
Slice, toasted---------- 1 slice----------------	20	24	65	2	1
Loaf, 2 lb----------------- 1 loaf-----------------	907	35	2,495	82	34
Slice (34 per loaf)------- 1 slice----------------	27	35	75	2	1
Slice, toasted---------- 1 slice----------------	23	24	75	2	1
Whole-wheat bread:					
Soft-crumb type:[38]					
Loaf, 1 lb----------------- 1 loaf-----------------	454	36	1,095	41	12
Slice (16 per loaf)------- 1 slice----------------	28	36	65	3	1
Slice, toasted---------- 1 slice----------------	24	24	65	3	1

Fatty Acids												
Saturated (total)	Unsaturated Oleic	Unsaturated Linoleic	Carbohydrate	Calcium	Phosphorus	Iron	Potassium	Vitamin A value	Thiamin	Riboflavin	Niacin	Ascorbic acid
(F)	(G)	(H)	(I)	(J)	(K)	(L)	(M)	(N)	(O)	(P)	(Q)	(R)
Grams	Grams	Grams	Grams	Milligrams	Milligrams	Milligrams	Milligrams	International units	Milligrams	Milligrams	Milligrams	Milligrams
.3	.2	.8	158	32	378	4.0	320	0	.24	.10	6.2	0
1.2	2.0	1.2	13	34	49	.4	33	Trace	.08	.08	.7	Trace
.6	1.1	.7	15	19	65	.6	32	Trace	.09	.08	.8	Trace
1.0	1.6	1.4	73	122	141	3.6	152	Trace	.35	.35	4.8	Trace
2.2	3.0	3.9	236	399	581	9.5	608	Trace	1.52	1.13	14.4	Trace
.1	.2	.2	13	22	32	.5	34	Trace	.08	.06	.8	Trace
3.2	4.7	4.6	251	195	386	10.0	408	Trace	1.80	1.10	15.0	Trace
.2	.4	.4	19	15	30	.8	32	Trace	.14	.08	1.2	Trace
.2	.3	.3	14	11	21	.6	23	Trace	.10	.06	.8	Trace
.6	.3	1.5	256	77	349	10.0	336	0	1.80	1.10	15.0	0
Trace	Trace	.1	17	5	23	.7	22	0	.12	.07	1.0	0
3.0	4.7	3.9	243	322	395	10.0	1,057	Trace	1.70	1.07	10.7	Trace
.2	.3	.2	13	18	22	.6	58	Trace	.09	.06	.6	Trace
.7	.5	2.2	236	340	667	9.1	658	0	1.35	.98	12.9	0
Trace	Trace	.1	13	19	37	.5	36	0	.07	.05	.7	0
.7	.5	2.4	241	381	1,039	11.8	2,059	0	1.30	.93	8.5	0
.1	Trace	.2	17	27	73	.8	145	0	.09	.07	.6	0
3.4	5.3	4.6	229	381	440	11.3	476	Trace	1.80	1.10	15.0	Trace
.2	.3	.3	13	21	24	.6	26	Trace	.10	.06	.8	Trace
.2	.3	.3	13	21	24	.6	26	Trace	.08	.06	.8	Trace
5.2	7.9	6.9	343	571	660	17.0	714	Trace	2.70	1.65	22.5	Trace
.2	.3	.3	14	24	27	.7	29	Trace	.11	.07	.9	Trace
.2	.3	.3	14	24	27	.7	29	Trace	.09	.07	.9	Trace
.2	.3	.3	15	25	29	.8	32	Trace	.12	.07	1.0	Trace
.3	.5	.5	23	38	44	1.1	47	Trace	.18	.11	1.5	Trace
3.9	5.9	5.2	228	435	463	11.3	549	Trace	1.80	1.10	15.0	Trace
.2	.3	.3	12	22	23	.6	28	Trace	.09	.06	.8	Trace
.2	.3	.3	12	22	23	.6	28	Trace	.07	.06	.8	Trace
7.7	11.8	10.4	455	871	925	22.7	1,097	Trace	3.60	2.20	30.0	Trace
.2	.3	.3	14	26	28	.7	33	Trace	.11	.06	.9	Trace
.2	.3	.3	14	26	28	.7	33	Trace	.09	.06	.9	Trace
2.2	2.9	4.2	224	381	1,152	13.6	1,161	Trace	1.37	.45	12.7	Trace
.1	.2	.2	14	24	71	.8	72	Trace	.09	.03	.8	Trace
.1	.2	.2	14	24	71	.8	72	Trace	.07	.03	.8	Trace

TABLE 2.— NUTRITIVE VALUES OF THE EDIBLE PART OF FOODS · Continued

(Dashes (—) denote lack of reliable data for a constituent believed to be present in measurable amount)

(A)		(B)	(C)	(D)	(E)
			NUTRIENTS IN INDICATED QUANTITY		
Firm-crumb type:[38]					
Loaf, 1 lb-----------------	1 loaf---------------	454	36	1,100	48	14
Slice (18 per loaf)-------	1 slice--------------	25	36	60	3	1
Slice, toasted----------	1 slice--------------	21	24	60	3	1
Breakfast cereals:					
Hot type, cooked:					
Farina, quick-cooking, en-riched.	1 cup---------------	245	89	105	3	Trace
Oatmeal or rolled oats--------	1 cup---------------	240	87	130	5	2
Wheat, rolled----------------	1 cup---------------	240	80	180	5	1
Wheat, whole-meal-------------	1 cup---------------	245	88	110	4	1
Ready-to-eat:					
Bran flakes (40% bran), added sugar, salt, iron, vitamins.	1 cup---------------	35	3	105	4	1
Bran flakes with raisins, add-ed sugar, salt, iron, vita-mins.	1 cup---------------	50	7	145	4	1
Corn flakes:					
Plain, added sugar, salt, iron, vitamins.	1 cup-----------------	25	4	95	2	Trace
Sugar-coated, added salt, iron, vitamins.	1 cup-----------------	40	2	155	2	Trace
Corn, puffed, plain, added sugar, salt, iron, vita-mins.	1 cup-----------------	20	4	80	2	1
Corn, shredded, added sugar, salt, iron, thiamin, niacin.	1 cup-----------------	25	3	95	2	Trace
Oats, puffed, added sugar, salt, minerals, vitamins.	1 cup-----------------	25	3	100	3	1
Rice, puffed:					
Plain, added iron, thiamin, niacin.	1 cup----------------	15	4	60	1	Trace
Presweetened, added salt, iron, vitamins.	1 cup----------------	28	3	115	1	0
Wheat flakes, added sugar, salt, iron, vitamins.	1 cup----------------	30	4	105	3	Trace
Wheat, puffed:					
Plain, added iron, thiamin, niacin.	1 cup----------------	15	3	55	2	Trace
Presweetened, added salt, iron, vitamins.	1 cup----------------	38	3	140	3	Trace
Wheat, shredded, plain-------	1 oblong biscuit or 1/2 cup spoon-size biscuits.	25	7	90	2	1
Wheat germ, without salt and sugar, toasted.	1 tbsp---------------	6	4	25	2	1
Buckwheat flour, light, sifted-	1 cup----------------	98	12	340	6	1
Bulgur, canned, seasoned---------	1 cup----------------	135	56	245	8	4
Cake icings. See Sugars and Sweets.					
Cakes made from cake mixes with enriched flour:[46]					
Angelfood:					
Whole cake (9 3/4-in diam. tube cake).	1 cake---------------	635	34	1,645	36	1
Piece, 1/12 of cake----------	1 piece--------------	53	34	135	3	Trace
Coffeecake:					
Whole cake (7 3/4 by 5 5/8 by 1 1/4 in).	1 cake---------------	430	30	1,385	27	41
Piece, 1/6 of cake-----------	1 piece--------------	72	30	230	5	7
Cupcakes, made with egg, milk, 2 1/2-in diam.:					
Without icing---------------	1 cupcake-------------	25	26	90	1	3
With chocolate icing--------	1 cupcake-------------	36	22	130	2	5
Devil's food with chocolate icing:					

(F)	(G)	(H)	(I)	(J)	(K)	(L)	(M)	(N)	(O)	(P)	(Q)	(R)
2.5	3.3	4.9	216	449	1,034	13.6	1,238	Trace	1.17	.54	12.7	Trace
.1	.2	.3	12	25	57	.8	68	Trace	.06	.03	.7	Trace
.1	.2	.3	12	25	57	.8	68	Trace	.05	.03	.7	Trace
Trace	Trace	.1	'22	147	[41]113	([42])	25	0	.12	.07	1.0	0
.4	.8	.9	23	22	137	1.4	146	0	.19	.05	.2	0
—	—	—	41	19	182	1.7	202	0	.17	.07	2.2	0
—	—	—	23	17	127	1.2	118	0	.15	.05	1.5	0
—	—	—	28	19	125	15.6	137	1,650	.41	.49	4.1	12
—	—	—	40	28	146	16.9	154	2,350	.58	.71	5.8	18
—	—	—	21	([43])	9	.6	30	1,180	.29	.35	2.9	9
—	—	—	37	1	10	1.0	27	1,880	.46	.56	4.6	14
—	—	—	16	4	18	2.3	—	940	.23	.28	2.3	7
—	—	—	22	1	10	.6	—	0	.11	.05	.5	0
—	—	—	19	44	102	2.9	—	1,180	.29	.35	2.9	9
—	—	—	13	3	14	.3	15	0	.07	.01	.7	0
—	—	—	26	3	14	[44]1.1	43	1,250	.38	.43	5.0	[45]15
—	—	—	24	12	83	([43])	81	1,410	.35	.42	3.5	11
—	—	—	12	4	48	.6	51	0	.08	.03	1.2	0
—	—	—	33	7	52	[44]1.6	63	1,680	.50	.57	6.7	[45]20
—	—	—	20	11	97	.9	87	0	.06	.03	1.1	0
—	—	—	3	3	70	.5	57	10	.11	.05	.3	1
.2	.4	.4	78	11	86	1.0	314	0	.08	.04	.4	0
—	—	—	44	27	263	1.9	151	0	.08	.05	4.1	0
—	—	—	377	603	756	2.5	381	0	.37	.95	3.6	0
—	—	—	32	50	63	.2	32	0	.03	.08	.3	0
11.7	16.3	8.8	225	262	748	6.9	469	690	.82	.91	7.7	1
2.0	2.7	1.5	38	44	125	1.2	78	120	.14	.15	1.3	Trace
.8	1.2	.7	14	40	59	.3	21	40	.05	.05	.4	Trace
2.0	1.6	.6	21	47	71	.4	42	60	.05	.06	.4	Trace

TABLE 2.— NUTRITIVE VALUES OF THE EDIBLE PART OF FOODS - Continued

(Dashes (—) denote lack of reliable data for a constituent believed to be present in measurable amount)

Foods, approximate measures, units, and weight (edible part unless footnotes indicate otherwise)		NUTRIENTS IN INDICATED QUANTITY			
		Water	Food energy	Pro-tein	Fat
(A)		(B)	(C)	(D)	(E)
	Grams	Per-cent	Cal-ories	Grams	Grams
Whole, 2 layer cake (8- or 9-in diam.). 1 cake	1,107	24	3,755	49	136
Piece, 1/16 of cake 1 piece	69	24	235	3	8
Cupcake, 2 1/2-in diam 1 cupcake	35	24	120	2	4
Gingerbread:					
Whole cake (8-in square) 1 cake	570	37	1,575	18	39
Piece, 1/9 of cake 1 piece	63	37	175	2	4
White, 2 layer with chocolate icing:					
Whole cake (8- or 9-in diam.) 1 cake	1,140	21	4,000	44	122
Piece, 1/16 of cake 1 piece	71	21	250	3	8
Yellow, 2 layer with chocolate icing:					
Whole cake (8- or 9-in diam.) 1 cake	1,108	26	3,735	45	125
Piece, 1/16 of cake 1 piece	69	26	235	3	8
Cakes made from home recipes using enriched flour:[47]					
Boston cream pie with custard filling:					
Whole cake (8-in diam.) 1 cake	825	35	2,490	41	78
Piece, 1/12 of cake 1 piece	69	35	210	3	6
Fruitcake, dark:					
Loaf, 1-lb (7 1/2 by 2 by 1 1/2 in). 1 loaf	454	18	1,720	22	69
Slice, 1/30 of loaf 1 slice	15	18	55	1	2
Plain, sheet cake:					
Without icing:					
Whole cake (9-in square) 1 cake	777	25	2,830	35	108
Piece, 1/9 of cake 1 piece	86	25	315	4	12
With uncooked white icing:					
Whole cake (9-in square) 1 cake	1,096	21	4,020	37	129
Piece, 1/9 of cake 1 piece	121	21	445	4	14
Pound:[49]					
Loaf, 8 1/2 by 3 1/2 by 3 1/4 in. 1 loaf	565	16	2,725	31	170
Slice, 1/17 of loaf 1 slice	33	16	160	2	10
Spongecake:					
Whole cake (9 3/4-in diam. tube cake). 1 cake	790	32	2,345	60	45
Piece, 1/12 of cake 1 piece	66	32	195	5	4
Cookies made with enriched flour:[50] [51]					
Brownies with nuts:					
Home-prepared, 1 3/4 by 1 3/4 by 7/8 in:					
From home recipe 1 brownie	20	10	95	1	6
From commercial recipe 1 brownie	20	11	85	1	4
Frozen, with chocolate icing,[52] 1 1/2 by 1 3/4 by 7/8 in. 1 brownie	25	13	105	1	5
Chocolate chip:					
Commercial, 2 1/4-in diam., 3/8 in thick. 4 cookies	42	3	200	2	9
From home recipe, 2 1/3-in diam. 4 cookies	40	3	205	2	12
Fig bars, square (1 5/8 by 1 5/8 by 3/8 in) or rectangular (1 1/2 by 1 3/4 by 1/2 in). 4 cookies	56	14	200	2	3
Gingersnaps, 2-in diam., 1/4 in thick. 4 cookies	28	3	90	2	2
Macaroons, 2 3/4-in diam., 1/4 in thick. 2 cookies	38	4	180	2	9
Oatmeal with raisins, 2 5/8-in diam., 1/4 in thick. 4 cookies	52	3	235	3	8

132

Fatty Acids												
Satu-rated (total)	Unsaturated		Carbo-hydrate	Calcium	Phos-phorus	Iron	Potas-sium	Vitamin A value	Thiamin	Ribo-flavin	Niacin	Ascorbic acid
	Oleic	Lino-leic										
(F)	(G)	(H)	(I)	(J)	(K)	(L)	(M)	(N)	(O)	(P)	(Q)	(R)
Grams	Grams	Grams	Grams	Milli-grams	Milli-grams	Milli-grams	Milli-grams	Inter-national units	Milli-grams	Milli-grams	Milli-grams	Milli-grams
50.0	44.9	17.0	645	653	1,162	16.6	1,439	1,660	1.06	1.65	10.1	1
3.1	2.8	1.1	40	41	72	1.0	90	100	.07	.10	.6	Trace
1.6	1.4	.5	20	21	37	.5	46	50	.03	.05	.3	Trace
9.7	16.6	10.0	291	513	570	8.6	1,562	Trace	.84	1.00	7.4	Trace
1.1	1.8	1.1	32	57	63	.9	173	Trace	.09	.11	.8	Trace
48.2	46.4	20.0	716	1,129	2,041	11.4	1,322	680	1.50	1.77	12.5	2
3.0	2.9	1.2	45	70	127	.7	82	40	.09	.11	.8	Trace
47.8	47.8	20.3	638	1,008	2,017	12.2	1,208	1,550	1.24	1.67	10.6	2
3.0	3.0	1.3	40	63	126	.8	75	100	.08	.10	.7	Trace
23.0	30.1	15.2	412	553	833	8.2	[48]734	1,730	1.04	1.27	9.6	2
1.9	2.5	1.3	34	46	70	.7	[48]61	140	.09	.11	.8	Trace
14.4	33.5	14.8	271	327	513	11.8	2,250	540	.72	.73	4.9	2
.5	1.1	.5	9	11	17	.4	74	20	.02	.02	.2	Trace
29.5	44.4	23.9	434	497	793	8.5	[48]614	1,320	1.21	1.40	10.2	2
3.3	4.9	2.6	48	55	88	.9	[48]68	150	.13	.15	1.1	Trace
42.2	49.5	24.4	694	548	822	8.2	[48]669	2,190	1.22	1.47	10.2	2
4.7	5.5	2.7	77	61	91	.8	[48]74	240	.14	.16	1.1	Trace
42.9	73.1	39.6	273	107	418	7.9	345	1,410	.90	.99	7.3	0
2.5	4.3	2.3	16	6	24	.5	20	80	.05	.06	.4	0
13.1	15.8	5.7	427	237	885	13.4	687	3,560	1.10	1.64	7.4	Trace
1.1	1.3	.5	36	20	74	1.1	57	300	.09	.14	.6	Trace
1.5	3.0	1.2	10	8	30	.4	38	40	.04	.03	.2	Trace
.9	1.4	1.3	13	9	27	.4	34	20	.03	.02	.2	Trace
2.0	2.2	.7	15	10	31	.4	44	50	.03	.03	.2	Trace
2.8	2.9	2.2	29	16	48	1.0	56	50	.10	.17	.9	Trace
3.5	4.5	2.9	24	14	40	.8	47	40	.06	.06	.5	Trace
.8	1.2	.7	42	44	34	1.0	111	60	.04	.14	.9	Trace
.7	1.0	.6	22	20	13	.7	129	20	.08	.06	.7	0
—	—	—	25	10	32	.3	176	0	.02	.06	.2	0
2.0	3.3	2.0	38	11	53	1.4	192	30	.15	.10	1.0	Trace

TABLE 2.– NUTRITIVE VALUES OF THE EDIBLE PART OF FOODS · Continued

(Dashes (−) denote lack of reliable data for a constituent believed to be present in measurable amount)

(A)		(B)	(C)	(D)	(E)
		NUTRIENTS IN INDICATED QUANTITY			
Plain, prepared from commercial chilled dough, 2 1/2-in diam., 1/4 in thick.	4 cookies ------------	48	5	240	2	12
Sandwich type (chocolate or vanilla), 1 3/4-in diam., 3/8 in thick.	4 cookies-------------	40	2	200	2	9
Vanilla wafers, 1 3/4-in diam., 1/4 in thick.	10 cookies------------	40	3	185	2	6
Cornmeal:						
Whole-ground, unbolted, dry form.	1 cup-----------------	122	12	435	11	5
Bolted (nearly whole-grain), dry form.	1 cup-----------------	122	12	440	11	4
Degermed, enriched:						
Dry form----------------------	1 cup-----------------	138	12	500	11	2
Cooked-----------------------	1 cup-----------------	240	88	120	3	Trace
Degermed, unenriched:						
Dry form----------------------	1 cup-----------------	138	12	500	11	2
Cooked-----------------------	1 cup-----------------	240	88	120	3	Trace
Crackers:[38]						
Graham, plain, 2 1/2-in square--	2 crackers------------	14	6	55	1	1
Rye wafers, whole-grain, 1 7/8 by 3 1/2 in.	2 wafers-------------	13	6	45	2	Trace
Saltines, enriched flour.	4 crackers -----------	11	4	50	1	1
Danish pastry (enriched flour), plain without fruit or nuts:[54]						
Ounce-------------------------	1 oz------------------	28	22	120	2	7
Doughnuts, enriched flour:[38]						
Cake type, plain, 2 1/2-in diam., 1 in high.	1 doughnut------------	25	24	100	1	5
Yeast-leavened, glazed, 3 3/4-in diam., 1 1/4 in high.	1 doughnut------------	50	26	205	3	11
Macaroni, enriched, cooked (cut lengths, elbows, shells):						
Firm stage (hot)---------------	1 cup-----------------	130	64	190	7	1
Tender stage:						
Cold macaroni-----------------	1 cup-----------------	105	73	115	4	Trace
Hot macaroni------------------	1 cup-----------------	140	73	155	5	1
Macaroni (enriched) and cheese:						
Canned[55]-----------------------	1 cup-----------------	240	80	230	9	10
From home recipe (served hot)[56]-	1 cup-----------------	200	58	430	17	22
Muffins made with enriched flour:[38]						
From home recipe:						
Blueberry, 2 3/8-in diam., 1 1/2 in high.	1 muffin-------------	40	39	110	3	4
Bran------------------------	1 muffin-------------	40	35	105	3	4
Corn (enriched degermed corn-meal and flour), 2 3/8-in diam., 1 1/2 in high.	1 muffin-------------	40	33	125	3	4
Plain, 3-in diam., 1 1/2 in high.	1 muffin-------------	40	38	120	3	4
From mix, egg, milk:						
Corn, 2 3/8-in diam., 1 1/2 in high.[58]	1 muffin-------------	40	30	130	3	4
Noodles (egg noodles), enriched, cooked.	1 cup-----------------	160	71	200	7	2
Noodles, chow mein, canned---------	1 cup-----------------	45	1	220	6	11
Pancakes, (4-in diam.):[38]						
Buckwheat, made from mix (with buckwheat and enriched flours), egg and milk added.	1 cake----------------	27	58	55	2	2
Plain:						
Made from home recipe using enriched flour.	1 cake----------------	27	50	60	2	2
Made from mix with enriched flour, egg and milk added.	1 cake----------------	27	51	60	2	2

(F)	(G)	(H)	(I)	(J)	(K)	(L)	(M)	(N)	(O)	(P)	(Q)	(R)
3.0	5.2	2.9	31	17	35	.6	23	30	.10	.08	.9	0
2.2	3.9	2.2	28	10	96	.7	15	0	.06	.10	.7	0
—	—	—	30	16	25	.6	29	50	.10	.09	.8	0
.5	1.0	2.5	90	24	312	2.9	346	[53]620	.46	.13	2.4	0
.5	.9	2.1	91	21	272	2.2	303	[53]590	.37	.10	2.3	0
.2	.4	.9	108	8	137	4.0	166	[53]610	.61	.36	4.8	0
Trace	.1	.2	26	2	34	1.0	38	[53]140	.14	.10	1.2	0
.2	.4	.9	108	8	137	1.5	166	[53]610	.19	.07	1.4	0
Trace	.1	.2	26	2	34	.5	38	[53]140	.05	.02	.2	0
.3	.5	.3	10	6	21	.5	55	0	.02	.08	.5	0
—	—	—	10	7	50	.5	78	0	.04	.03	.2	0
.3	.5	.4	8	2	10	.5	13	0	.05	.05	.4	0
2.0	2.7	1.4	13	14	31	.5	32	90	.08	.08	.7	Trace
1.2	2.0	1.1	13	10	48	.4	23	20	.05	.05	.4	Trace
3.3	5.8	3.3	22	16	33	.6	34	25	.10	.10	.8	0
—	—	—	39	14	85	1.4	103	0	.23	.13	1.8	0
—	—	—	24	8	53	.9	64	0	.15	.08	1.2	0
—	—	—	32	11	70	1.3	85	0	.20	.11	1.5	0
4.2	3.1	1.4	26	199	182	1.0	139	260	.12	.24	1.0	Trace
8.9	8.8	2.9	40	362	322	1.8	240	860	.20	.40	1.8	Trace
1.1	1.4	.7	17	34	53	.6	46	90	.09	.10	.7	Trace
1.2	1.4	.8	17	57	162	1.5	172	90	.07	.10	1.7	Trace
1.2	1.6	.9	19	42	68	.7	54	[57]120	.10	.10	.7	Trace
1.0	1.7	1.0	17	42	60	.6	50	40	.09	.12	.9	Trace
1.2	1.7	.9	20	96	152	.6	44	[57]100	.08	.09	.7	Trace
—	—	—	37	16	94	1.4	70	110	.22	.13	1.9	0
—	—	—	26	—	—	—	—	—	—	—	—	—
.8	.9	.4	6	59	91	.4	66	60	.04	.05	.2	Trace
.5	.8	.5	9	27	38	.4	33	30	.06	.07	.5	Trace
.7	.7	.3	9	58	70	.3	42	70	.04	.06	.2	Trace

TABLE 2.– NUTRITIVE VALUES OF THE EDIBLE PART OF FOODS - Continued

(Dashes (—) denote lack of reliable data for a constituent believed to be present in measurable amount)

Foods, approximate measures, units, and weight (edible part unless footnotes indicate otherwise)			Water	Food energy	Pro-tein	Fat
(A)			(B)	(C)	(D)	(E)
		Grams	Per-cent	Cal-ories	Grams	Grams
Pies, piecrust made with enriched flour, vegetable shortening (9-in diam.):						
Apple:						
Whole-------------------------	1 pie----------------	945	48	2,420	21	105
Sector, 1/7 of pie-------------	1 sector-------------	135	48	345	3	15
Banana cream:						
Whole-------------------------	1 pie----------------	910	54	2,010	41	85
Sector, 1/7 of pie-------------	1 sector-------------	130	54	285	6	12
Blueberry:						
Whole-------------------------	1 pie----------------	945	51	2,285	23	102
Sector, 1/7 of pie-------------	1 sector-------------	135	51	325	3	15
Cherry:						
Whole-------------------------	1 pie----------------	945	47	2,465	25	107
Sector, 1/7 of pie-------------	1 sector-------------	135	47	350	4	15
Custard:						
Whole-------------------------	1 pie----------------	910	58	1,985	56	101
Sector, 1/7 of pie-------------	1 sector-------------	130	58	285	8	14
Lemon meringue:						
Whole-------------------------	1 pie----------------	840	47	2,140	31	86
Sector, 1/7 of pie-------------	1 sector-------------	120	47	305	4	12
Peach:						
Whole-------------------------	1 pie----------------	945	48	2,410	24	101
Sector, 1/7 of pie-------------	1 sector-------------	135	48	345	3	14
Pecan:						
Whole-------------------------	1 pie----------------	825	20	3,450	42	189
Sector, 1/7 of pie-------------	1 sector-------------	118	20	495	6	27
Pumpkin:						
Whole-------------------------	1 pie----------------	910	59	1,920	36	102
Sector, 1/7 of pie-------------	1 sector-------------	130	59	275	5	15
Piecrust (home recipe) made with enriched flour and vegetable shortening, baked.	1 pie shell, 9-in diam.-------	180	15	900	11	60
Piecrust mix with enriched flour and vegetable shortening, 10-oz pkg. prepared and baked.	2-crust pie, 9-in diam. --------	320	19	1,485	20	93
Pizza (cheese) baked, 4 3/4-in sector; 1/8 of 12-in diam. pie.[19]	1 sector-------------	60	45	145	6	4
Popcorn, popped:						
Plain, large kernel------------	1 cup----------------	6	4	25	1	Trace
With oil (coconut) and salt added, large kernel.	1 cup----------------	9	3	40	1	2
Pretzels, made with enriched flour:						
Dutch, twisted, 2 3/4 by 2 5/8 in.	1 pretzel------------	16	5	60	2	1
Thin, twisted, 3 1/4 by 2 1/4 by 1/4 in.	10 pretzels----------	60	5	235	6	3
Stick, 2 1/4 in long----------	10 pretzels----------	3	5	10	Trace	Trace
Rice, white, enriched:						
Instant, ready-to-serve, hot---	1 cup----------------	165	73	180	4	Trace
Long grain:						
Raw------------------------	1 cup----------------	185	12	670	12	1
Cooked, served hot-----------	1 cup----------------	205	73	225	4	Trace
Parboiled:						
Raw------------------------	1 cup----------------	185	10	685	14	1
Cooked, served hot-----------	1 cup----------------	175	73	185	4	Trace
Rolls, enriched:[38]						
Commercial:						
Brown-and-serve (12 per 12-oz pkg.), browned.	1 roll---------------	26	27	85	2	2

Saturated (total) (F) Grams	Unsaturated Oleic (G) Grams	Unsaturated Linoleic (H) Grams	Carbohydrate (I) Grams	Calcium (J) Milligrams	Phosphorus (K) Milligrams	Iron (L) Milligrams	Potassium (M) Milligrams	Vitamin A value (N) International units	Thiamin (O) Milligrams	Riboflavin (P) Milligrams	Niacin (Q) Milligrams	Ascorbic acid (R) Milligrams
27.0	44.5	25.2	360	76	208	6.6	756	280	1.06	.79	9.3	9
3.9	6.4	3.6	51	11	30	.9	108	40	.15	.11	1.3	2
26.7	33.2	16.2	279	601	746	7.3	1,847	2,280	.77	1.51	7.0	9
3.8	4.7	2.3	40	86	107	1.0	264	330	.11	.22	1.0	1
24.8	43.7	25.1	330	104	217	9.5	614	280	1.03	.80	10.0	28
3.5	6.2	3.6	47	15	31	1.4	88	40	.15	.11	1.4	4
28.2	45.0	25.3	363	132	236	6.6	992	4,160	1.09	.84	9.8	Trace
4.0	6.4	3.6	52	19	34	.9	142	590	.16	.12	1.4	Trace
33.9	38.5	17.5	213	874	1,028	8.2	1,247	2,090	.79	1.92	5.6	0
4.8	5.5	2.5	30	125	147	1.2	178	300	.11	.27	.8	0
26.1	33.8	16.4	317	118	412	6.7	420	1,430	.61	.84	5.2	25
3.7	4.8	2.3	45	17	59	1.0	60	200	.09	.12	.7	4
24.8	43.7	25.1	361	95	274	8.5	1,408	6,900	1.04	.97	14.0	28
3.5	6.2	3.6	52	14	39	1.2	201	990	.15	.14	2.0	4
27.8	101.0	44.2	423	388	850	25.6	1,015	1,320	1.80	.95	6.9	Trace
4.0	14.4	6.3	61	55	122	3.7	145	190	.26	.14	1.0	Trace
37.4	37.5	16.6	223	464	628	7.3	1,456	22,480	.78	1.27	7.0	Trace
5.4	5.4	2.4	32	66	90	1.0	208	3,210	.11	.18	1.0	Trace
14.8	26.1	14.9	79	25	90	3.1	89	0	.47	.40	5.0	0
22.7	39.7	23.4	141	131	272	6.1	179	0	1.07	.79	9.9	0
1.7	1.5	.6	22	86	89	1.1	67	230	.16	.18	1.6	4
Trace	.1	.2	5	1	17	.2	—	—	—	.01	.1	0
1.5	.2	.2	5	1	19	.2	—	—	—	.01	.2	0
—	—	—	12	4	21	.2	21	0	.05	.04	.7	0
—	—	—	46	13	79	.9	78	0	.20	.15	2.5	0
—	—	—	2	1	4	Trace	4	0	.01	.01	.1	0
Trace	Trace	Trace	40	5	31	1.3	—	0	.21	([59])	1.7	0
.2	.2	.2	149	44	174	5.4	170	0	.81	.06	6.5	0
.1	.1	.1	50	21	57	1.8	57	0	.23	.02	2.1	0
.2	.1	.2	150	111	370	5.4	278	0	.81	.07	6.5	0
.1	.1	.1	41	33	100	1.4	75	0	.19	.02	2.1	0
.4	.7	.5	14	20	23	.5	25	Trace	.10	.06	.9	Trace

TABLE 2.– NUTRITIVE VALUES OF THE EDIBLE PART OF FOODS - Continued

(Dashes (−) denote lack of reliable data for a constituent believed to be present in measurable amount)

(A)		(B)	(C)	(D)	(E)
		NUTRIENTS IN INDICATED QUANTITY			
Cloverleaf or pan, 2 1/2-in diam., 2 in high.	1 roll--------------	28	31	85	2	2
Frankfurter and hamburger (8 per 11 1/2-oz pkg.).	1 roll--------------	40	31	120	3	2
Hard, 3 3/4-in diam., 2 in high.	1 roll--------------	50	25	155	5	2
Hoagie or submarine, 11 1/2 by 3 by 2 1/2 in.	1 roll--------------	135	31	390	12	4
Spaghetti, enriched, cooked:						
Firm stage, "al dente," hot.	1 cup--------------	130	64	190	7	1
Tender stage, served hot-------	1 cup--------------	140	73	155	5	1
Spaghetti (enriched) in tomato sauce with cheese:						
From home recipe---------------	1 cup--------------	250	77	260	9	9
Canned-------------------------	1 cup--------------	250	80	190	6	2
Spaghetti (enriched) with meat balls and tomato sauce:						
From home recipe---------------	1 cup--------------	248	70	330	19	12
Canned-------------------------	1 cup--------------	250	78	260	12	10
Waffles, made with enriched flour, 7-in diam.:[38]						
From home recipe---------------	1 waffle------------	75	41	210	7	7
From mix, egg and milk added---	1 waffle------------	75	42	205	7	8
Wheat flours:						
All-purpose or family flour, enriched:						
Sifted, spooned---------------	1 cup--------------	115	12	420	12	1
Unsifted, spooned-------------	1 cup--------------	125	12	455	13	1
Cake or pastry flour, enriched, sifted, spooned.	1 cup--------------	96	12	350	7	1
Self-rising, enriched, unsifted, spooned.	1 cup--------------	125	12	440	12	1
Whole-wheat, from hard wheats, stirred.	1 cup--------------	120	12	400	16	2
LEGUMES (DRY), NUTS, SEEDS; RELATED PRODUCTS						
Almonds, shelled:						
Chopped -----------------------	1 cup--------------	130	5	775	24	70
Slivered, not pressed down	1 cup--------------	115	5	690	21	62
Beans, dry:						
Common varieties:						
Cooked, drained:						
Great Northern-------------	1 cup--------------	180	69	210	14	1
Pea (navy)-----------------	1 cup--------------	190	69	225	15	1
Lima, cooked, drained-----------	1 cup--------------	190	64	260	16	1
Blackeye peas, dry, cooked (with residual cooking liquid).	1 cup--------------	250	80	190	13	1
Brazil nuts, shelled	1 oz----------------	28	5	185	4	19
Cashew nuts, roasted in oil-------	1 cup--------------	140	5	785	24	64
Coconut meat, fresh:						
Shredded or grated, not pressed down.	1 cup--------------	80	51	275	3	28
Filberts (hazelnuts), chopped	1 cup--------------	115	6	730	14	72
Lentils, whole, cooked-----------	1 cup--------------	200	72	210	16	Trace
Peanuts, roasted in oil, salted (whole, halves, chopped).	1 cup--------------	144	2	840	37	72
Peanut butter--------------------	1 tbsp-------------	16	2	95	4	8
Peas, split, dry, cooked----------	1 cup--------------	200	70	230	16	1
Pecans, chopped or pieces	1 cup--------------	118	3	810	11	84
Sunflower seeds, dry, hulled------	1 cup--------------	145	5	810	35	69
Walnuts:						
Black:						
Chopped or broken kernels-----	1 cup--------------	125	3	785	26	74
Ground (finely)---------------	1 cup--------------	80	3	500	16	47
Persian or English, chopped	1 cup--------------	120	4	780	18	77

(F)	(G)	(H)	(I)	(J)	(K)	(L)	(M)	(N)	(O)	(P)	(Q)	(R)
.4	.6	.4	15	21	24	.5	27	Trace	.11	.07	.9	Trace
.5	.8	.6	21	30	34	.8	38	Trace	.16	.10	1.3	Trace
.4	.6	.5	30·	24	46	1.2	49	Trace	.20	.12	1.7	Trace
.9	1.4	1.4	75	58	115	3.0	122	Trace	.54	.32	4.5	Trace
——	——	——	39	14	85	1.4	103	0	.23	.13	1.8	0
——	——	——	32	11	70	1.3	85	0	.20	.11	1.5	0
2.0	5.4	.7	37	80	135	2.3	408	1,080	.25	.18	2.3	13
.5	.3	.4	39	40	88	2.8	303	930	.35	.28	4.5	10
3.3	6.3	.9	39	124	236	3.7	665	1,590	.25	.30	4.0	22
2.2	3.3	3.9	29	53	113	3.3	245	1,000	.15	.18	2.3	5
2.3	2.8	1.4	28	85	130	1.3	109	250	.17	.23	1.4	Trace
2.8	2.9	1.2	27	179	257	1.0	146	170	.14	.22	.9	Trace
.2	.1	.5	88	18	100	3.3	109	0	.74	.46	6.1	0
.2	.1	.5	95	20	109	3.6	119	0	.80	.50	6.6	0
.1	.1	.3	76	16	70	2.8	91	0	.61	.38	5.1	0
.2	.1	.5	93	331	583	3.6	——	0	.80	.50	6.6	0
.4	.2	1.0	85	49	446	4.0	444	0	.66	.14	5.2	0
5.6	47.7	12.8	25	304	655	6.1	1,005	0	.31	1.20	4.6	Trace
5.0	42.2	11.3	22	269	580	5.4	889	0	.28	1.06	4.0	Trace
——	——	——	38	90	266	4.9	749	0	.25	.13	1.3	0
——	——	——	40	95	281	5.1	790	0	.27	.13	1.3	0
——	——	——	49	55	293	5.9	1,163	——	.25	.11	1.3	——
——	——	——	35	43	238	3.3	573	30	.40	.10	1.0	——
4.8	6.2	7.1	3	53	196	1.0	203	Trace	..27	.03	.5	——
12.9	36.8	10.2	41	53	522	5.3	650	140	.60	.35	2.5	——
24.8	1.6	.5	8	10	76	1.4	205	0	.04	.02	.4	2
5.1	55.2	7.3	19	240	388	3.9	810	——	.53	——	1.0	Trace
——	——	——	39	50	238	4.2	498	40	.14	.12	1.2	0
13.7	33.0	20.7	27	107	577	3.0	971	——	.46	.19	24.8	0
1.5	3.7	2.3	3	9	61	.3	100	——	.02	.02	2.4	0
——	——	——	42	22	178	3.4	592	80	.30	.18	1.8	——
7.2	50.5	20.0	17	86	341	2.8	712	150	1.01	.15	1.1	2
8.2	13.7	43.2	29	174	1,214	10.3	1,334	70	2.84	.33	7.8	——
6.3	13.3	45.7	19	Trace	713	7.5	575	380	.28	.14	.9	——
4.0	8.5	29.2	12	Trace	456	4.8	368	240	.18	.09	.6	——
8.4	11.8	42.2	19	119	456	3.7	540	40	.40	.16	1.1	2

Foods, approximate measures, units, and weight (edible part unless footnotes indicate otherwise)		Water	Food energy	Pro-tein	Fat
(A)		(B)	(C)	(D)	(E)
	Grams	Per-cent	Cal-ories	Grams	Grams

SUGARS AND SWEETS

Foods, approximate measures, units, and weight		Grams	Per-cent	Cal-ories	Grams	Grams
Cake icings:						
Boiled, white:						
Plain--------------------------	1 cup------------------	94	18	295	1	0
Uncooked:						
Chocolate made with milk and butter.	1 cup------------------	275	14	1,035	9	38
Creamy fudge from mix and water.	1 cup------------------	245	15	830	7	16
White------------------------	1 cup------------------	319	11	1,200	2	21
Candy:						
Caramels, plain or chocolate----	1 oz-------------------	28	8	115	1	3
Chocolate:						
Milk, plain------------------	1 oz-------------------	28	1	145	2	9
Semisweet, small pieces	1 cup ------------------	170	1	860	7	61
Chocolate-coated peanuts--------	1 oz-------------------	28	1	160	5	12
Fondant, uncoated (mints, candy corn, other).	1 oz-------------------	28	8	105	Trace	1
Fudge, chocolate, plain---------	1 oz-------------------	28	8	115	1	3
Hard-------------------------	1 oz-------------------	28	1	110	0	Trace
Marshmallows-----------------	1 oz-------------------	28	17	90	1	Trace
Honey, strained or extracted------	1 tbsp------------------	21	17	65	Trace	0
Jams and preserves---------------	1 tbsp------------------	20	29	55	Trace	Trace
	1 packet---------------	14	29	40	Trace	Trace
Jellies-------------------------	1 tbsp------------------	18	29	50	Trace	Trace
	1 packet_____	14	29	40	Trace	Trace
Sirups:						
Chocolate-flavored sirup or topping:						
Thin type--------------------	1 fl oz or 2 tbsp------	38	32	90	1	1
Fudge type--------------------	1 fl oz or 2 tbsp------	38	25	125	2	5
Molasses, cane:						
Light (first extraction)------	1 tbsp------------------	20	24	50	—	—
Blackstrap (third extraction)-	1 tbsp------------------	20	24	45	—	—
Table blends, chiefly corn, light and dark.	1 tbsp------------------	21	24	60	0	0
Sugars:						
Brown, pressed down-------------	1 cup------------------	220	2	820	0	0
White:						
Granulated--------------------	1 cup------------------	200	1	770	0	0
	1 tbsp------------------	12	1	45	0	0
Powdered, sifted, spooned into cup.	1 cup------------------	100	1	385	0	0

VEGETABLE AND VEGETABLE PRODUCTS

Foods, approximate measures, units, and weight		Grams	Per-cent	Cal-ories	Grams	Grams
Asparagus, green:						
Cooked, drained:						
Cuts and tips, 1 1/2- to 2-in lengths:						
From raw---------------------	1 cup------------------	145	94	30	3	Trace
From frozen------------------	1 cup------------------	180	93	40	6	Trace
Spears, 1/2-in diam. at base:						
From raw---------------------	4 spears--------------	60	94	10	1	Trace
From frozen------------------	4 spears--------------	60	92	15	2	Trace
Canned, spears, 1/2-in diam. at base.	4 spears--------------	80	93	15	2	Trace
Beans:						
Lima, immature seeds, frozen, cooked, drained:						
Thick-seeded types (Fordhooks)	1 cup------------------	170	74	170	10	Trace
Thin-seeded types (baby limas)	1 cup------------------	180	69	210	13	Trace

	Fatty Acids											
Saturated (total)	Unsaturated Oleic	Linoleic	Carbohydrate	Calcium	Phosphorus	Iron	Potassium	Vitamin A value	Thiamin	Riboflavin	Niacin	Ascorbic acid
(F)	(G)	(H)	(I)	(J)	(K)	(L)	(M)	(N)	(O)	(P)	(Q)	(R)
Grams	Grams	Grams	Grams	Milligrams	Milligrams	Milligrams	Milligrams	International units	Milligrams	Milligrams	Milligrams	Milligrams
0	0	0	75	2	2	Trace	17	0	Trace	.03	Trace	0
23.4	11.7	1.0	185	165	305	3.3	536	580	.06	.28	.6	1
5.1	6.7	3.1	183	96	218	2.7	238	Trace	.05	.20	.7	Trace
12.7	5.1	.5	260	48	38	Trace	57	860	Trace	.06	Trace	Trace
1.6	1.1	.1	22	42	35	.4	54	Trace	.01	.05	.1	Trace
5.5	3.0	.3	16	65	65	.3	109	80	.02	.10	.1	Trace
36.2	19.8	1.7	97	51	255	4.4	553	30	.02	.14	.9	0
4.0	4.7	2.1	11	33	84	.4	143	Trace	.10	.05	2.1	Trace
.1	.3	.1	25	4	2	.3	1	0	Trace	Trace	Trace	0
1.3	1.4	.6	21	22	24	.3	42	Trace	.01	.03	.1	Trace
—	—	—	28	6	2	.5	1	0	0	0	0	0
—	—	—	23	5	2	.5	2	0	0	Trace	Trace	0
0	0	0	17	1	1	.1	11	0	Trace	.01	.1	Trace
—	—	—	14	4	2	.2	18	Trace	Trace	.01	Trace	Trace
—	—	—	10	3	1	.1	12	Trace	Trace	Trace	Trace	Trace
—	—	—	13	4	1	.3	14	Trace	Trace	.01	Trace	1
—	—	—	10	3	1	.2	11	Trace	Trace	Trace	Trace	1
.5	.3	Trace	24	6	35	.6	106	Trace	.01	.03	.2	0
3.1	1.6	.1	20	48	60	.5	107	60	.02	.08	.2	Trace
—	—	—	13	33	9	.9	183	—	.01	.01	Trace	—
—	—	—	11	137	17	3.2	585	—	.02	.04	.4	—
0	0	0	15	9	3	.8	1	0	0	0	0	0
0	0	0	212	187	42	7.5	757	0	.02	.07	.4	0
0	0	0	199	0	0	.2	6	0	0	0	0	0
0	0	0	12	0	0	Trace	Trace	0	0	0	0	0
0	0	0	100	0	0	.1	3	0	0	0	0	0
—	—	—	5	30	73	.9	265	1,310	.23	.26	2.0	38
—	—	—	6	40	115	2.2	396	1,530	.25	.23	1.8	41
—	—	—	2	13	30	.4	110	540	.10	.11	.8	16
—	—	—	2	13	40	.7	143	470	.10	.08	.7	16
—	—	—	3	15	42	1.5	133	640	.05	.08	.6	12
—	—	—	32	34	153	2.9	724	390	.12	.09	1.7	29
—	—	—	40	63	227	4.7	709	400	.16	.09	2.2	22

TABLE 2.– NUTRITIVE VALUES OF THE EDIBLE PART OF FOODS - Continued

(Dashes (−) denote lack of reliable data for a constituent believed to be present in measurable amount)

(A)		(B)	(C)	(D)	(E)
		NUTRIENTS IN INDICATED QUANTITY			
Snap:					
Green:					
Cooked, drained:					
From raw (cuts and French style).	1 cup----------------	125	92	30	2	Trace
From frozen:					
Cuts---------------------	1 cup----------------	135	92	35	2	Trace
French style------------	1 cup----------------	130	92	35	2	Trace
Canned, drained solids (cuts).	1 cup----------------	135	92	30	2	Trace
Yellow or wax:					
Cooked, drained:					
From raw (cuts and French style).	1 cup----------------	125	93	30	2	Trace
From frozen (cuts)--------	1 cup----------------	135	92	35	2	Trace
Canned, drained solids (cuts).	1 cup----------------	135	92	30	2	Trace
Bean sprouts (mung):					
Raw--------------------------	1 cup----------------	105	89	35	4	Trace
Cooked, drained----------------	1 cup----------------	125	91	35	4	Trace
Beets:					
Cooked, drained, peeled:					
Whole beets, 2-in diam.-------	2 beets--------------	100	91	30	1	Trace
Diced or sliced--------------	1 cup----------------	170	91	55	2	Trace
Canned, drained solids:					
Whole beets, small-----------	1 cup----------------	160	89	60	2	Trace
Diced or sliced--------------	1 cup----------------	170	89	65	2	Trace
Beet greens, leaves and stems, cooked, drained.	1 cup----------------	145	94	25	2	Trace
Blackeye peas, immature seeds, cooked and drained:					
From raw----------------------	1 cup----------------	165	72	180	13	1
From frozen-------------------	1 cup----------------	170	66	220	15	1
Broccoli, cooked, drained:					
From raw:					
Stalk, medium size-----------	1 stalk--------------	180	91	45	6	1
Stalks cut into 1/2-in pieces-	1 cup----------------	155	91	40	5	Trace
From frozen:					
Stalk, 4 1/2 to 5 in long-----	1 stalk--------------	30	91	10	1	Trace
Chopped----------------------	1 cup----------------	185	92	50	5	1
Brussels sprouts, cooked, drained:					
From raw, 7-8 sprouts (1 1/4- to 1 1/2-in diam.).	1 cup----------------	155	88	55	7	1
From frozen--------------------	1 cup----------------	155	89	50	5	Trace
Cabbage:					
Common varieties:					
Raw:					
Coarsely shredded or sliced-	1 cup----------------	70	92	15	1	Trace
Finely shredded or chopped--	1 cup----------------	90	92	20	1	Trace
Cooked, drained--------------	1 cup----------------	145	94	30	2	Trace
Red, raw, coarsely shredded or sliced.	1 cup----------------	70	90	20	1	Trace
Savoy, raw, coarsely shredded or sliced.	1 cup----------------	70	92	15	2	Trace
Cabbage, celery (also called pe-tsai or wongbok), raw, 1-in pieces.	1 cup----------------	75	95	10	1	Trace
Cabbage, white mustard (also called bokchoy or pakchoy), cooked, drained.	1 cup----------------	170	95	25	2	Trace
Carrots:					
Raw, without crowns and tips, scraped:					
Whole, 7 1/2 by 1 1/8 in, or strips, 2 1/2 to 3 in long.	1 carrot ------------	72	88	30	1	Trace

142

(F)	(G)	(H)	(I)	(J)	(K)	(L)	(M)	(N)	(O)	(P)	(Q)	(R)
—	—	—	7	63	46	.8	189	680	.09	.11	.6	15
—	—	—	8	54	43	.9	205	780	.09	.12	.5	7
—	—	—	8	49	39	1.2	177	690	.08	.10	.4	9
—	—	—	7	61	34	2.0	128	630	.04	.07	.4	5
—	—	—	6	63	46	.8	189	290	.09	.11	.6	16
—	—	—	8	47	42	.9	221	140	.09	.11	.5	8
—	—	—	7	61	34	2.0	128	140	.04	.07	.4	7
—	—	—	7	20	67	1.4	234	20	.14	.14	.8	20
—	—	—	7	21	60	1.1	195	30	.11	.13	.9	8
—	—	—	7	14	23	.5	208	20	.03	.04	.3	6
—	—	—	12	24	39	.9	354	30	.05	.07	.5	10
—	—	—	14	30	29	1.1	267	30	.02	.05	.2	5
—	—	—	15	32	31	1.2	284	30	.02	.05	.2	5
—	—	—	5	144	36	2.8	481	7,400	.10	.22	.4	22
—	—	—	30	40	241	3.5	625	580	.50	.18	2.3	28
—	—	—	40	43	286	4.8	573	290	.68	.19	2.4	15
—	—	—	8	158	112	1.4	481	4,500	.16	.36	1.4	162
—	—	—	7	136	96	1.2	414	3,880	.14	.31	1.2	140
—	—	—	1	12	17	.2	66	570	.02	.03	.2	22
—	—	—	9	100	104	1.3	392	4,810	.11	.22	.9	105
—	—	—	10	50	112	1.7	423	810	.12	.22	1.2	135
—	—	—	10	33	95	1.2	457	880	.12	.16	.9	126
—	—	—	4	34	20	.3	163	90	.04	.04	.02	33
—	—	—	5	44	26	.4	210	120	.05	.05	.3	42
—	—	—	6	64	29	.4	236	190	.06	.06	.4	48
—	—	—	5	29	25	.6	188	30	.06	.04	.3	43
—	—	—	3	47	38	.6	188	140	.04	.06	.2	39
—	—	—	2	32	30	.5	190	110	.04	.03	.5	19
—	—	—	4	252	56	1.0	364	5,270	.07	.14	1.2	26
—	—	—	7	27	26	.5	246	7,930	.04	.04	.4	6

TABLE 2.— NUTRITIVE VALUES OF THE EDIBLE PART OF FOODS - Continued

(Dashes (—) denote lack of reliable data for a constituent believed to be present in measurable amount)

Foods, approximate measures, units, and weight (edible part unless footnotes indicate otherwise)		Water	Food energy	Pro- tein	Fat
(A)		(B)	(C)	(D)	(E)
		Grams	Per- cent	Cal- ories	Grams	Grams

Grated------------------------ 1 cup-----------------	110	88	45	1	Trace
Cooked (crosswise cuts), drained 1 cup-----------------	155	91	50	1	Trace
Canned:					
Sliced, drained solids-------- 1 cup-----------------	155	91	45	1	Trace
Strained or junior (baby food) 1 oz -----------------	28	92	10	Trace	Trace
Cauliflower:					
Raw, chopped-------------------- 1 cup-----------------	115	91	31	3	Trace
Cooked, drained:					
From raw (flower buds)-------- 1 cup-----------------	125	93	30	3	Trace
From frozen (flowerets)------- 1 cup-----------------	180	94	30	3	Trace
Celery, Pascal type, raw:					
Stalk, large outer, 8 by 1 1/2 1 stalk------------- in, at root end.	40	94	5	Trace	Trace
Pieces, diced------------------- 1 cup-----------------	120	94	20	1	Trace
Collards, cooked, drained:					
From raw (leaves without stems)- 1 cup-----------------	190	90	65	7	1
From frozen (chopped)----------- 1 cup-----------------	170	90	50	5	1
Corn, sweet:					
Cooked, drained:					
From raw, ear 5 by 1 3/4 in--- 1 ear[61]--------------	140	74	70	2	1
From frozen:					
Ear, 5 in long-------------- 1 ear[61]--------------	229	73	120	4	1
Kernels-------------------- 1 cup-----------------	165	77	130	5	1
Canned:					
Cream style------------------- 1 cup-----------------	256	76	210	5	2
Whole kernel:					
Vacuum pack---------------- 1 cup-----------------	210	76	175	5	1
Wet pack, drained solids---- 1 cup-----------------	165	76	140	4	1
Cucumber slices, 1/8 in thick (large, 2 1/8-in diam.; small, 1 3/4-in diam.):					
With peel---------------------- 6 large -------------	28	95	5	Trace	Trace
Without peel------------------- 6 1/2 large or 9 small pieces.	28	96	5	Trace	Trace
Dandelion greens, cooked, drained- 1 cup-----------------	105	90	35	2	1
Endive, curly (including escarole), 1 cup----------------- raw, small pieces.	50	93	10	1	Trace
Kale, cooked, drained:					
From raw (leaves without stems 1 cup----------------- and midribs).	110	88	45	5	1
From frozen (leaf style)-------- 1 cup-----------------	130	91	40	4	1
Lettuce, raw:					
Butterhead, as Boston types:					
Head, 5-in diam-------------- 1 head[63]-------------	220	95	25	2	Trace
Leaves----------------------- 1 outer or 2 inner or 3 heart leaves.	15	95	Trace	Trace	Trace
Crisphead, as Iceberg:					
Head, 6-in diam-------------- 1 head[64]-------------	567	96	70	5	1
Wedge, 1/4 of head----------- 1 wedge--------------	135	96	20	1	Trace
Pieces, chopped or shredded--- 1 cup-----------------	55	96	5	Trace	Trace
Looseleaf (bunching varieties 1 cup----------------- including romaine or cos), chopped or shredded pieces.	55	94	10	1	Trace
Mushrooms, raw, sliced or chopped- 1 cup-----------------	70	90	20	2	Trace
Mustard greens, without stems and 1 cup----------------- midribs, cooked, drained.	140	93	30	3	1
Okra pods, 3 by 5/8 in, cooked---- 10 pods--------------	106	91	30	2	Trace

144

	Fatty Acids											
Satu-rated (total)	Unsaturated		Carbo-hydrate	Calcium	Phos-phorus	Iron	Potas-sium	Vitamin A value	Thiamin	Ribo-flavin	Niacin	Ascorbic acid
	Oleic	Lino-leic										
(F)	(G)	(H)	(I)	(J)	(K)	(L)	(M)	(N)	(O)	(P)	(Q)	(R)
Grams	Grams	Grams	Grams	Milli-grams	Milli-grams	Milli-grams	Milli-grams	Inter-national units	Milli-grams	Milli-grams	Milli-grams	Milli-grams
—	—	—	11	41	40	.8	375	12,100	.07	.06	.7	9
—	—	—	11	51	48	.9	344	16,280	.08	.08	.8	9
—	—	—	10	47	34	1.1	186	23,250	.03	.05	.6	3
—	—	—	2	7	6	.1	51	3,690	.01	.01	.1	1
—	—	—	6	29	64	1.3	339	70	.13	.12	.8	90
—	—	—	5	26	53	.9	258	80	.11	.10	.8	69
—	—	—	6	31	68	.9	373	50	.07	.09	.7	74
—	—	—	2	16	11	.1	136	110	.01	.01	.1	4
—	—	—	5	47	34	.4	409	320	.04	.04	.4	11
—	—	—	10	357	99	1.5	498	14,820	.21	.38	2.3	144
—	—	—	10	299	87	1.7	401	11,560	.10	.24	1.0	56
—	—	—	16	2	69	.5	151	[62]310	.09	.08	1.1	7
—	—	—	27	4	121	1.0	291	[62]440	.18	.10	2.1	9
—	—	—	31	5	120	1.3	304	[62]580	.15	.10	2.5	8
—	—	—	51	8	143	1.5	248	[62]840	.08	.13	2.6	13
—	—	—	43	6	153	1.1	204	[62]740	.06	.13	2.3	11
—	—	—	33	8	81	.8	160	[62]580	.05	.08	1.5	7
—	—	—	1	7	8	.3	45	70	.01	.01	.1	3
—	—	—	1	5	5	.1	45	Trace	.01	.01	.1	3
—	—	—	7	147	44	1.9	244	12,290	.14	.17	—	19
—	—	—	2	41	27	.9	147	1,650	.04	.07	.3	5
—	—	—	7	206	64	1.8	243	9,130	.11	.20	1.8	102
—	—	—	7	157	62	1.3	251	10,660	.08	.20	.9	49
—	—	—	4	57	42	3.3	430	1,580	.10	.10	.5	13
—	—	—	Trace	5	4	.3	40	150	.01	.01	Trace	1
—	—	—	16	108	118	2.7	943	1,780	.32	.32	1.6	32
—	—	—	4	27	30	.7	236	450	.08	.08	.4	8
— —	—	—	2	11	12	.3	96	180	.03	.03	.2	3
—	—	—	2	37	14	.8	145	1.050	.03	.04	.2	10
—	—	—	3	4	81	.6	290	Trace	.07	.32	2.9	2
—	—	—	6	193	45	2.5	308	8,120	.11	.20	.8	67
—	—	—	6	98	43	.5	184	520	.14	.19	1.0	21

TABLE 2.– NUTRITIVE VALUES OF THE EDIBLE PART OF FOODS - Continued

(Dashes (—) denote lack of reliable data for a constituent believed to be present in measurable amount)

(A)		(B)	(C)	(D)	(E)
		NUTRIENTS IN INDICATED QUANTITY			
Onions:					
Mature:					
Raw:					
Chopped--------------------	1 cup----------------	170	89	65	3	Trace
Sliced----------------------	1 cup----------------	115	89	45	2	Trace
Cooked (whole or sliced), drained.	1 cup----------------	210	92	60	3	Trace
Young green, bulb (3/8 in diam.) and white portion of top.	6 onions-------------	30	88	15	Trace	Trace
Parsley, raw, chopped-------------	1 tbsp---------------	4	85	Trace	Trace	Trace
Parsnips, cooked (diced or 2-in lengths).	1 cup----------------	155	82	100	2	1
Peas, green:					
Canned:					
Whole, drained solids---------	1 cup----------------	170	77	150	8	1
Strained (baby food)----------	1 oz ----------------	28	86	15	1	Trace
Frozen, cooked, drained----------	1 cup----------------	160	82	110	8	Trace
Peppers, hot, red, without seeds, dried (ground chili powder, added seasonings).	1 tsp---------------	2	9	5	Trace	Trace
Peppers, sweet (about 5 per lb, whole), stem and seeds removed:					
Raw----------------------------	1 pod----------------	74	93	15	1	Trace
Cooked, boiled, drained--------	1 pod----------------	73	95	15	1	Trace
Potatoes, cooked:					
Baked, peeled after baking (about 2 per lb, raw).	1 potato-------------	156	75	145	4	Trace
Boiled (about 3 per lb, raw):					
Peeled after boiling----------	1 potato-------------	137	80	105	3	Trace
Peeled before boiling--------	1 potato-------------	135	83	90	3	Trace
French-fried, strip, 2 to 3 1/2 in long:					
Prepared from raw-------------	10 strips------------	50	45	135	2	7
Frozen, oven heated-----------	10 strips------------	50	53	110	2	4
Hashed brown, prepared from frozen.	1 cup----------------	155	56	345	3	18
Mashed, prepared from—					
Raw:					
Milk added------------------	1 cup----------------	210	83	135	4	2
Milk and butter added-------	1 cup----------------	210	80	195	4	9
Dehydrated flakes (without milk), water, milk, butter, and salt added.	1 cup----------------	210	79	195	4	7
Potato chips, 1 3/4 by 2 1/2 in oval cross section.	10 chips-------------	20	2	115	1	8
Potato salad, made with cooked salad dressing.	1 cup----------------	250	76	250	7	7
Pumpkin, canned-------------------	1 cup----------------	245	90	80	2	1
Radishes, raw (prepackaged) stem ends, rootlets cut off.	4 radishes-----------	18	95	5	Trace	Trace
Sauerkraut, canned, solids and liquid.	1 cup----------------	235	93	40	2	Trace
Spinach:					
Raw, chopped---------------------	1 cup----------------	55	91	15	2	Trace
Cooked, drained:					
From raw----------------------	1 cup----------------	180	92	40	5	1
From frozen:					
Chopped-----------------------	1 cup----------------	205	92	45	6	1
Leaf--------------------------	1 cup----------------	190	92	45	6	1
Canned, drained solids----------	1 cup----------------	205	91	50	6	1
Squash, cooked:					
Summer (all varieties), diced, drained.	1 cup----------------	210	96	30	2	Trace
Winter (all varieties), baked, mashed.	1 cup----------------	205	81	130	4	1

146

(F)	(G)	(H)	(I)	(J)	(K)	(L)	(M)	(N)	(O)	(P)	(Q)	(R)
—	—	—	15	46	61	.9	267	[65]Trace	.05	.07	.3	17
—	—	—	10	31	41	.6	181	[65]Trace	.03	.05	.2	12
—	—	—	14	50	61	.8	231	[65]Trace	.06	.06	.4	15
—	—	—	3	12	12	.2	69	Trace	.02	.01	.1	8
—	—	— Trace	7	2	.2	25	300	Trace	.01	Trace	6	
—	—	—	23	70	96	.9	587	50	.11	.12	.2	16
—	—	—	29	44	129	3.2	163	1,170	.15	.10	1.4	14
—	—	—	3	3	18	.3	28	140	.02	.03	.3	3
—	—	—	19	30	138	3.0	216	960	.43	.14	2.7	21
—	—	—	1	5	4	.3	20	1,300	Trace	.02	.2	Trace
—	—	—	4	7	16	.5	157	310	.06	.06	.4	94
—	—	—	3	7	12	.4	109	310	.05	.05	.4	70
—	—	—	33	14	101	1.1	782	Trace	.15	.07	2.7	31
—	—	—	23	10	72	.8	556	Trace	.12	.05	2.0	22
—	—	—	20	8	57	.7	385	Trace	.12	.05	1.6	22
1.7	1.2	3.3	18	8	56	.7	427	Trace	.07	.04	1.6	11
1.1	.8	2.1	17	5	43	.9	326	Trace	.07	.01	1.3	11
4.6	3.2	9.0	45	28	78	1.9	439	Trace	.11	.03	1.6	12
.7	.4	Trace	27	50	103	.8	548	40	.17	.11	2.1	21
5.6	2.3	.2	26	50	101	.8	525	360	.17	.11	2.1	19
3.6	2.1	.2	30	65	99	.6	601	270	.08	.08	1.9	11
2.1	1.4	4.0	10	8	28	.4	226	Trace	.04	.01	1.0	3
2.0	2.7	1.3	41	80	160	1.5	798	350	.20	.18	2.8	28
—	—	—	19	61	64	1.0	588	15,680	.07	.12	1.5	12
—	—	—	1	5	6	.2	58	Trace	.01	.01	.1	5
—	—	—	9	85	42	1.2	329	120	.07	.09	.5	33
—	—	—	2	51	28	1.7	259	4,460	.06	.11	.3	28
—	—	—	6	167	68	4.0	583	14,580	.13	.25	.9	50
—	—	—	8	232	90	4.3	683	16,200	.14	.31	.8	39
—	—	—	7	200	84	4.8	688	15,390	.15	.27	1.0	53
—	—	—	7	242	53	5.3	513	16,400	.04	.25	.6	29
—	—	—	7	53	53	.8	296	820	.11	.17	1.7	21
—	—	—	32	57	98	1.6	945	8,610	.10	.27	1.4	27

TABLE 2.– NUTRITIVE VALUES OF THE EDIBLE PART OF FOODS - Continued

(Dashes (—) denote lack of reliable data for a constituent believed to be present in measurable amount)

Foods, approximate measures, units, and weight (edible part unless footnotes indicate otherwise) (A)			Water (B)	Food energy (C)	Protein (D)	Fat (E)
			NUTRIENTS IN INDICATED QUANTITY			
		Grams	*Percent*	*Calories*	*Grams*	*Grams*
Sweetpotatoes:						
Cooked (raw, 5 by 2 in; about 2 1/2 per lb):						
Baked in skin, peeled--------	1 potato------------	114	64	160	2	1
Boiled in skin, peeled--------	1 potato------------	151	71	170	3	1
Candied, 2 1/2 by 2-in piece----	1 piece-------------	105	60	175	1	3
Canned:						
Solid pack (mashed)----------	1 cup---------------	255	72	275	5	1
Vacuum pack, piece 2 3/4 by 1 in.	1 piece-------------	40	72	45	1	Trace
Tomatoes:						
Raw, 2 3/5-in diam. (3 per 12 oz pkg.).	1 tomato[66]----------	135	94	25	1	Trace
Canned, solids and liquid------	1 cup---------------	241	94	50	2	Trace
Tomato catsup-------------------	1 cup---------------	273	69	290	5	1
	1 tbsp--------------	15	69	15	Trace	Trace
Tomato juice, canned:						
Cup-----------------------------	1 cup---------------	243	94	45	2	Trace
Glass (6 fl oz)----------------	1 glass-------------	182	94	35	2	Trace
Turnips, cooked, diced-----------	1 cup---------------	155	94	35	1	Trace
Turnip greens, cooked, drained:						
From raw (leaves and stems)-----	1 cup---------------	145	94	30	3	Trace
From frozen (chopped)----------	1 cup---------------	165	93	40	4	Trace
Vegetables, mixed, frozen, cooked	1 cup---------------	182	83	115	6	1
MISCELLANEOUS ITEMS						
Baking powders for home use:						
Sodium aluminum sulfate:						
With monocalcium phosphate monohydrate.	1 tsp---------------	3.0	2	5	Trace	Trace
With monocalcium phosphate monohydrate, calcium sulfate.	1 tsp---------------	2.9	1	5	Trace	Trace
Straight phosphate-------------	1 tsp---------------	3.8	2	5	Trace	Trace
Low sodium---------------------	1 tsp---------------	4.3	2	5	Trace	Trace
Barbecue sauce------------------	1 cup---------------	250	81	230	4	17
Beverages, alcoholic:						
Beer----------------------------	12 fl oz------------	360	92	150	1	0
Gin, rum, vodka, whisky:						
80-proof---------------------	1 1/2-fl oz jigger---	42	67	95	—	—
86-proof---------------------	1 1/2-fl oz jigger---	42	64	105	—	—
90-proof---------------------	1 1/2-fl oz jigger---	42	62	110	—	—
Wines:						
Dessert----------------------	3 1/2-fl oz glass----	103	77	140	Trace	0
Table------------------------	3 1/2-fl oz glass----	102	86	85	Trace	0
Beverages, carbonated, sweetened, nonalcoholic:						
Carbonated water---------------	12 fl oz------------	366	92	115	0	0
Cola type-----------------------	12 fl oz------------	369	90	145	0	0
Fruit-flavored sodas and Tom Collins mixer.	12 fl oz------------	372	88	170	0	0
Ginger ale---------------------	12 fl oz------------	366	92	115	0	0
Root beer----------------------	12 fl oz------------	370	90	150	0	0
Chocolate:						
Bitter or baking---------------	1 oz----------------	28	2	145	3	15
Semisweet, see Candy, chocolate						

	Fatty Acids											
Satu-rated (total)	Unsaturated		Carbo-hydrate	Calcium	Phos-phorus	Iron	Potas-sium	Vitamin A value	Thiamin	Ribo-flavin	Niacin	Ascorbic acid
	Oleic	Lino-leic										
(F)	(G)	(H)	(I)	(J)	(K)	(L)	(M)	(N)	(O)	(P)	(Q)	(R)
Grams	Grams	Grams	Grams	Milli-grams	Milli-grams	Milli-grams	Milli-grams	Inter-national units	Milli-grams	Milli-grams	Milli-grams	Milli-grams
—	—	—	37	46	66	1.0	342	9,230	.10	.08	.8	25
—	—	—	40	48	71	1.1	367	11,940	.14	.09	.9	26
2.0	.8	.1	36	39	45	.9	200	6,620	.06	.04	.4	11
—	—	—	63	64	105	2.0	510	19,890	.13	.10	1.5	36
—	—	—	10	10	16	.3	80	3,120	.02	.02	.2	6
—	—	—	6	16	33	.6	300	1,110	.07	.05	.9	[6][7]28
—	—	—	10	[6][8]14	46	1.2	523	2,170	.12	.07	1.7	41
—	—	—	69	60	137	2.2	991	3,820	.25	.19	4.4	41
—	—	—	4	3	8	.1	54	210	.01	.01	.2	2
—	—	—	10	17	44	2.2	552	1,940	.12	.07	1.9	39
—	—	—	8	13	33	1.6	413	1,460	.09	.05	1.5	29
—	—	—	8	54	37	.6	291	Trace	.06	.08	.5	34
—	—	—	5	252	49	1.5	—	8,270	.15	.33	.7	68
—	—	—	6	195	64	2.6	246	11,390	.08	.15	.7	31
—	—	—	24	46	115	2.4	348	9,010	.22	.13	2.0	15
0	0	0	1	58	87	—	5	0	0	0	0	0
0	0	0	1	183	45	—	—	0	0	0	0	0
0	0	0	1	239	359	—	6	0	0	0	0	0
0	0	0	2	207	314	—	471	0	0	0	0	0
2.2	4.3	10.0	20	53	50	2.0	435	900	.03	.03	.8	13
0	0	0	14	18	108	Trace	90	—	.01	.11	2.2	—
0	0	0	Trace	—	—	—	1	—	—	—	—	—
0	0	0	Trace	—	—	—	1	—	—	—	—	—
0	0	0	Trace	—	—	—	1	—	—	—	—	—
0	0	0	8	8	—	—	77	—	.01	.02	.2	—
0	0	0	4	9	10	.4	94	—	Trace	.01	.1	—
0	0	0	29	—	—	—	—	0	0	0	0	0
0	0	0	37	—	—	—	—	0	0	0	0	0
0	0	0	45	—	—	—	—	0	0	0	0	0
0	0	0	29	—	—	—	0	0	0	0	0	0
0	0	0	39	—	—	—	0	0	0	0	0	0
8.9	4.9	.4	8	22	109	1.9	235	20	.01	.07	.4	0

TABLE 2.— NUTRITIVE VALUES OF THE EDIBLE PART OF FOODS - Continued

(Dashes (—) denote lack of reliable data for a constituent believed to be present in measurable amount)

(A)		(B)	(C)	(D)	(E)
		NUTRIENTS IN INDICATED QUANTITY			
Gelatin, dry----------------------	1 7-g envelope------------ 7	13	25	6	Trace
Gelatin dessert prepared with gelatin dessert powder and water.	1 cup---------------------240	84	140	4	0
Mustard, prepared, yellow---------	1 tsp or individual serving pouch or cup. 5	80	5	Trace	Trace
Olives, pickled, canned:					
Green---------------------------	4 medium or 3 extra large or 2 giant.[69] 16	78	15	Trace	2
Ripe, Mission-------------------	3 small or 2 large[69]------ 10	73	15	Trace	2
Pickles, cucumber:					
Dill, medium, whole, 3 3/4 in long, 1 1/4-in diam.	1 pickle------------------ 65	93	5	Trace	Trace
Fresh-pack, slices 1 1/2-in diam., 1/4 in thick.	2 slices------------------ 15	79	10	Trace	Trace
Sweet, gherkin, small, whole, about 2 1/2 in long, 3/4-in diam.	1 pickle------------------ 15	61	20	Trace	Trace
Relish, finely chopped, sweet---	1 tbsp-------------------- 15	63	20	Trace	Trace
Popsicle, 3-fl oz size------------	1 popsicle--------------- 95	80	70	0	0
Soups:					
Canned, condensed:					
Prepared with equal volume of milk:					
Cream of chicken-------------	1 cup--------------------- 245	85	180	7	10
Cream of mushroom-----------	1 cup--------------------- 245	83	215	7	14
Tomato----------------------	1 cup--------------------- 250	84	175	7	7
Prepared with equal volume of water:					
Bean with pork--------------	1 cup--------------------- 250	84	170	8	6
Beef broth, bouillon, consomme.	1 cup--------------------- 240	96	30	5	0
Beef noodle-----------------	1 cup--------------------- 240	93	65	4	3
Clam chowder, Manhattan type (with tomatoes, without milk).	1 cup--------------------- 245	92	80	2	3
Cream of chicken-------------	1 cup--------------------- 240	92	95	3	6
Cream of mushroom-----------	1 cup--------------------- 240	90	135	2	10
Minestrone------------------	1 cup--------------------- 245	90	105	5	3
Split pea--------------------	1 cup--------------------- 245	85	145	9	3
Tomato----------------------	1 cup--------------------- 245	91	90	2	3
Vegetable beef--------------	1 cup--------------------- 245	92	80	5	2
Vegetarian------------------	1 cup--------------------- 245	92	80	2	2
Dehydrated:					
Bouillon cube, 1/2 in----------	1 cube------------------- 4	4	5	1	Trace
Mixes:					
Unprepared:					
Onion----------------------	1 1/2-oz pkg------------ 43	3	150	6	5
Prepared with water:					
Chicken noodle-------------	1 cup--------------------- 240	95	55	2	1
Onion---------------------	1 cup--------------------- 240	96	35	1	1
Tomato vegetable with noodles.	1 cup--------------------- 240	93	65	1	1
Vinegar, cider---------------------	1 tbsp------------------- 15	94	Trace	Trace	0
White sauce, medium, with enriched flour.	1 cup------------------- 250	73	405	10	31
Yeast:					
Baker's, dry, active-------------	1 pkg-------------------- 7	5	20	3	Trace
Brewer's, dry--------------------	1 tbsp-------------------- 8	5	25	3	Trace

(F)	(G)	(H)	(I)	(J)	(K)	(L)	(M)	(N)	(O)	(P)	(Q)	(R)
0	0	0	0	—	—	—	—	—	—	—	—	—
0	0	0	34	—	—	—	—	—	—	—	—	—
—	—	—	Trace	4	4	.1	7	—	—	—	—	—
.2	1.2	.1	Trace	8	2	.2	7	40	—	—	—	—
.2	1.2	.1	Trace	9	1	.1	2	10	Trace	Trace	—	—
—	—	—	1	17	14	.7	130	70	Trace	.01	Trace	4
—	—	—	3	5	4	.3	—	20	Trace	Trace	Trace	1
—	—	—	5	2	2	.2	—	10	Trace	Trace	Trace	1
—	—	—	5	3	2	.1	—	—	—	—	—	—
0	0	0	18	0	—	Trace	—	0	0	0	0	0
4.2	3.6	1.3	15	172	152	.5	260	610	.05	.27	.7	2
5.4	2.9	4.6	16	191	169	.5	279	250	.05	.34	.7	1
3.4	1.7	1.0	23	168	155	.8	418	1,200	.10	.25	1.3	15
1.2	1.8	2.4	22	63	128	2.3	395	650	.13	.08	1.0	3
0	0	0	3	Trace	31	.5	130	Trace	Trace	.02	1.2	—
.6	.7	.8	7	7	48	1.0	77	50	.05	.07	1.0	Trace
.5	.4	1.3	12	34	47	1.0	184	880	.02	.02	1.0	—
1.6	2.3	1.1	8	24	34	.5	79	410	.02	.05	.5	Trace
2.6	1.7	4.5	10	41	50	.5	98	70	.02	.12	.7	Trace
.7	.9	1.3	14	37	59	1.0	314	2,350	.07	.05	1.0	—
1.1	1.2	.4	21	29	149	1.5	270	440	.25	.15	1.5	1
.5	.5	1.0	16	15	34	.7	230	1,000	.05	.05	1.2	12
—	—	—	10	12	49	.7	162	2,700	.05	.05	1.0	—
—	—	—	13	20	39	1.0	172	2,940	.05	.05	1.0	—
—	—	—	Trace	—	—	—	4	—	—	—	—	—
1.1	2.3	1.0	23	42	49	.6	238	30	.05	.03	.3	6
—	—	—	8	7	19	.2	19	50	.07	.05	.5	Trace
—	—	—	6	10	12	.2	58	Trace	Trace	Trace	Trace	2
—	—	—	12	7	19	.2	29	480	.05	.02	.5	5
0	0	0	1	1	1	.1	15	—	—	—	—	—
19.3	7.8	.8	22	288	233	.5	348	1,150	.12	.43	.7	2
—	—	—	3	3	90	1.1	140	Trace	.16	.38	2.6	Trace
—	—	—	3	[70]17	140	1.4	152	Trace	1.25	.34	3.0	Trace

Footnotes

[1] Vitamin A value is largely from beta-carotene used for coloring.

[2] Applies to product without added vitamin A. With added vitamin A, value is 500 International Units (I.U.).

[3] Applies to product without vitamin A added.

[4] Applies to product with added vitamin A. Without added vitamin A, value is 20 International Units (I.U.).

[5] Yields 1 qt of fluid milk when reconstituted according to package directions.

[6] Applies to product with added vitamin A.

[7] Weight applies to product with label claim of 1 1/3 cups equal 3.2 oz.

[8] Applies to products made from thick shake mixes and that do not contain added ice cream. Products made from milk shake mixes are higher in fat and usually contain added ice cream.

[9] Content of fat, vitamin A, and carbohydrate varies. Consult the label when precise values are needed for special diets.

[10] Applies to product made with milk containing no added vitamin A.

[11] Based on year-round average.

[12] Based on average vitamin A content of fortified margarine. Federal specifications for fortified margarine require a minimum of 15,000 International Units (I.U.) of vitamin A per pound.

[13] Fatty acid values apply to product made with regular-type margarine.

[14] Dipped in egg, milk or water, and breadcrumbs; fried in vegetable shortening.

[15] If bones are discarded, value for calcium will be greatly reduced.

[16] Dipped in egg, breadcrumbs, and flour or batter.

[17] Prepared with tuna, celery, salad dressing (mayonnaise type), pickle, onion, and egg.

[18] Outer layer of fat on the cut was removed to within approximately 1/2 in of the lean. Deposits of fat within the cut were not removed.

[19] Crust made with vegetable shortening and enriched flour.

[20] Regular-type margarine used.

[21] Value varies widely.

[22] About one-fourth of the outer layer of fat on the cut was removed. Deposits of fat within the cut were not removed.

[23] Vegetable shortening used.

[24] Also applies to pasteurized apple cider.

[25] Applies to product without added ascorbic acid. For value of product with added ascorbic acid, refer to label.

[26] Based on product with label claim of 45% of U.S. RDA in 6 fl oz.

[27] Based on product with label claim of 100% of U.S. RDA in 6 fl oz.

[28] Weight includes peel and membranes between sections.

[29] For white-fleshed varieties, value is about 20 International Units (I.U.) per cup; for red-fleshed varieties, 1,080 I.U.

[30] Weight includes seeds. Without seeds, weight of the edible portion is 57 g.

[31] Applies to product without added ascorbic acid. With added ascorbic acid, based on claim that 6 fl oz of reconstituted juice contain 45% or 50% of the U.S. RDA, value in milligrams is 108 or 120 for a 6-fl oz can, 36 or 40 for 1 cup of diluted juice.

[32] For products with added thiamin and riboflavin but without added ascorbic acid, values in milligrams would be 0.60 for thiamin, 0.80 for riboflavin, and trace for ascorbic acid. For products with only ascorbic acid added, value varies with the brand. Consult the label.

[33] Weight includes rind.

[34] Represents yellow-fleshed varieties. For white-fleshed varieties, value is 50 International Units (I.U.) for 1 peach, 90 I.U. for 1 cup of slices.

[35] Value represents products with added ascorbic acid. For products without added ascorbic acid, value in milligrams is 116 for a 10-oz container, 103 for 1 cup.

[36] Weight includes pits.

[37] Weight includes rind and seeds. Without rind and seeds, weight of the edible portion is 426 g.

[38] Made with vegetable shortening.

[39] Applies to product made with white cornmeal. With yellow cornmeal, value is 30 International Units (I.U.).

[40] Applies to white varieties. For yellow varieties, value is 150 International Units (I.U.).

[41] Applies to products that do not contain di-sodium phosphate. If di-sodium phosphate is an ingredient, value is 162 mg.

[42] Value may range from less than 1 mg to about 8 mg depending on the brand. Consult the label.

[43] Value varies with the brand. Consult the label.

[44] Value varies with the brand. Consult the label.

[45] Applies to product with added ascorbic acid. Without added ascorbic acid, value is trace.

[46] Excepting angelfood cake, cakes were made from mixes containing vegetable shortening; icings, with butter.

152

[47]Excepting spongecake, vegetable shortening used for cake portion; butter, for icing. If butter or margarine used for cake portion, vitamin A values would be higher.

[48]Applies to product made with a sodium aluminum-sulfate type baking powder. With a low-sodium type baking powder containing potassium, value would be about twice the amount shown.

[49]Equal weights of flour, sugar, eggs, and vegetable shortening.

[50]Products are commercial unless otherwise specified.

[51]Made with enriched flour and vegetable shortening except for macaroons which do not contain flour or shortening.

[52]Icing made with butter.

[53]Applies to yellow varieties; white varieties contain only a trace.

[54]Contains vegetable shortening and butter.

[55]Made with corn oil.

[56]Made with regular margarine.

[57]Applies to product made with yellow cornmeal.

[58]Made with enriched degermed cornmeal and enriched flour.

[59]Product may or may not be enriched with riboflavin. Consult the label.

[60]Value varies with the brand. Consult the label.

[61]Weight includes cob.

[62]Based on yellow varieties. For white varieties, value is trace.

[63]Weight includes refuse of outer leaves and core. Without these parts, weight is 163 g.

[64]Weight includes core. Without core, weight is 539 g.

[65]Value based on white-fleshed varieties.

[66]Weight includes cores and stem ends. Without these parts, weight is 123 g.

[67]Based on year-round average. For tomatoes marketed from November through May, value is about 12 mg; from June through October, 32 mg.

[68]Applies to product without calcium salts added. Value for products with calcium salts added may be as much as 63 mg for whole tomatoes, 241 mg for cut forms.

[69]Weight includes pits. Without pits, weight is 13 g for item 701, 9 g for item 702.

[70]Value may vary from 6 to 60 mg.

INDEX